DOCUMENTS OF MODERN HISTORY

General Editors:

A. G. Dickens
The Director, Institute of Historical Research, University of London

Alun Davies
Professor of Modern History, University College, Swansea

DOCUMENTS OF MODERN HISTORY

ENGLISH COLONIZATION OF NORTH AMERICA

edited by

Louis B. Wright and Elaine W. Fowler

New York · St. Martin's Press

© Louis B. Wright and Elaine W. Fowler 1968

First published 1968

*First published in
the United States of America in 1968
by St. Martin's Press, Inc,
175 Fifth Avenue, New York, New York
First Published in Great Britain by
Edward Arnold (Publishers) Ltd*

Library of Congress Catalog Card Number: 68-29505

Printed in Great Britain by
Robert Cunningham and Sons Ltd, Alva

CONTENTS

IV RELIGION AND EDUCATION

V ECONOMIC DEVELOPMENT

VI RELATIONS WITH THE INDIANS

PREFACE

The documents reprinted here are designed to provide provocative suggestions of the main lines of development in the thirteen British colonies in North America that became the United States. The space limitations of this volume prevent a more comprehensive treatment. We have attempted to select documents that are significant yet brief enough to fit into the space allotted us.

Readers who wish a more comprehensive treatment of colonial documents are referred to *English Historical Documents*: *American Colonial Documents to 1776*, ed. Merrill Jensen (London, 1955). The present editors wish to express their own indebtedness to Professor Jensen.

We also wish to thank Miss Barbara Babcock for her assistance in the preparation of the manuscript.

Louis B. Wright
Elaine W. Fowler

Washington, 31 October 1967

INTRODUCTION

Colonial Civilization in British North America

The story of the development of the thirteen British colonies in North America that eventually became the United States offers many incidents and episodes up to that time new in the experience of the English people. With the exception of some slight experience in making settlements in Ireland, England in the seventeenth century had no knowledge of the problems of overseas possessions. It had never sent out colonies, and the closest contact with colonial possessions that most literate Englishmen had at the time of the settlement of Jamestown came from reading about the colonial activities of the Greeks and the Romans.

Englishmen, of course, had been aware for many years of the progress made by Spain and Portugal in establishing themselves overseas, in the New World, in Africa, and in the Far East. Merchants and adventurers yearned for part of the profits that flowed into Iberian coffers from the conquest of Mexico and Peru, from Mexican mines, and from the Portuguese trade with Africa and India. The influx of precious metal affected all of western Europe, but England was a late-comer in seeking direct access to overseas wealth.

The reasons for this delay are not hard to discern. Spain and Portugal had early obtained a monopoly of the new lands by decree of Pope Alexander VI, later modified by the Treaty of Tordesillas. Since England was not yet hostile to Spain, she could not dispute Spain's rights and it was not until well into the second half of the sixteenth century that Englishmen began seriously to wage a campaign of propaganda for overseas expansion.

That does not mean that nothing was done to establish some claim to a portion of the New World. Henry VII, after declining to back Columbus' first voyage of discovery, finally was persuaded to send out John Cabot in 1497 on an expedition to North America that gave England at least a shadowy claim to a part of that continent.

As hostility toward Spain increased in the second half of the sixteenth century, a few Englishmen began to urge the necessity of establishing colonies or at least operational bases in North America. The chief propagandist was Richard Hakluyt, preacher, compiler of the famous voyages, a work that he intended to be helpful to English explorers and adventurers overseas.

Not all Englishmen agreed that colonial enterprise would be a good thing. Although Raleigh, Walsingham, Leicester, and a group of their associates were expansionists, they had to overcome the opposition of cautious men like William Cecil, Lord Burghley, who believed that England's prosperity depended upon trade across the Channel and the maintenance of peace with England's Continental neighbours as long as that was possible. Queen Elizabeth was willing to support Francis Drake's expedition that circumnavigated the globe and preyed on Spanish towns on the Pacific coast of America, but she warned that on no account was 'my Lord Treasurer' (Burghley) to be informed about preparations for the expedition.

The first serious effort at colonial settlement began with a patent issued to Humphrey Gilbert in 1578 to discover and settle lands not already claimed by any Christian prince. Under that patent Gilbert proclaimed the Queen's possession of Newfoundland in 1583. After Gilbert's death at sea, Hakluyt continued his propaganda for colonial settlement in North America and Raleigh began an active campaign to establish settlements in the New World. He received a charter in 1584 that was almost the same in words and intent as that issued to Gilbert. He also sent out an exploring expedition under Philip Amadas and Arthur Barlow, who brought back enthusiastic reports about the coast of what is now North Carolina. To the whole land, Raleigh gave the name Virginia in honour of the Virgin Queen.

Raleigh's efforts to establish a colony failed, partly because of poor preparation and the inexperience of the colonists, partly because the distractions of the Spanish Armada in 1588 prevented support of the infant colony, which disappeared leaving one of the mysteries of early American history, the mystery of what happened to 'the lost colony'.

With the establishment of peace with Spain after the accession of James I, the way was open for another effort to found a colony in North America, provided it did not encroach on Spain's area of potential occupation. Once more colonists sought the shores of Virginia, this time in the Chesapeake Bay area, and their settlement, made in 1607 at Jamestown, after many vicissitudes, managed to survive.

The first permanent English colony was founded under a charter issued by James I on 10 April 1606. Fashioned after the joint-stock charters used in England and in other European countries to carry on trade overseas, the first Virginia charter differed in that the sovereign reserved to himself certain rights, particularly that of appointing royal councillors who would retain control of the operation of the colony. This council would appoint local councils in the colony. The charter also provided for two groups of colonizers, the London Company and the Plymouth Company. This first charter proved unsatisfactory to the ordinary investors in the company, for it gave them little control over company affairs. Consequently, on 23 May 1609, a second Virginia charter was issued, more nearly like the normal trading company charters. This charter abandoned the use of a royal council, turned over control to a council and treasurer chosen from the investors by the Crown, gave the company ownership of the land, and separated the Plymouth Company from the corporate body. But this charter also proved unsatisfactory because it still left to the Crown the authority of appointing officials. The third charter, issued on 12 March 1612, was modelled on a trading company charter analogous to that of the East India Company. It gave the stockholders the right to elect officers and conduct the affairs of the colony, providing that its regulations and laws did not contravene the laws of England. This type of charter became the normal charter for colonial enterprise. Virginia operated under this charter until it was annulled in 1624 and the colony was taken over as a royal possession.

Under the Virginia charter of 1612, the management of the colony continued in the hands of a council elected by the stockholders but the council maintained its headquarters in London. The charter issued to the Massachusetts Bay Company in 1629 was similar to the Virginia Company charter of 1612. But the principal stockholders and members of the council of the Massachusetts Bay Company emigrated to New England and brought their charter with them, an action that the government did not anticipate. That made the Massachusetts Bay Company virtually a self-governing and self-perpetuating body with little interference from London. But since it placed the government in the hands of a relatively small body of Puritan stockholders and their heirs, it was far from democratic in its operation and led to much complaint on both sides of the Atlantic.

Another type of colony was founded under a proprietary charter issued to a magnate who received a grant of land from the sovereign and could dispose of it as he saw fit. Maryland, the first proprietary colony, was founded under a charter granted to Cecil Calvert, second

Baron Baltimore, on 20 June 1632. This type of charter was a reversion to the feudal system, the charter of Maryland being modelled after the customs and conditions of the County Palatine of Durham. Under this system, the proprietor owed to the sovereign only his loyalty and nominal dues. The Maryland charter prescribed that the proprietor must deliver to the King 'two Indian arrows of these parts . . . at the said Castle of Windsor, every year on Tuesday of Easter Week' and turn over 'the fifth part of all gold and silver ore which shall happen from time to time to be found within the aforesaid limits'. Other proprietary colonies were Carolina, New York (and the region to the south that became New Jersey), Pennsylvania, and Georgia. The charter given William Penn contained limitations not found in the charters given to Calvert, the proprietors of Carolina, and the Duke of York (the first proprietor of New York and New Jersey). The proprietary grant to the trustees of Georgia in 1732 specified that the grant was good for only twenty years after which the control would be vested in the Crown.

The charter system of incorporating colonies proved unsatisfactory and Parliament attempted from time to time to rescind the charters or to alter them. By the time of the Revolution, all of the colonies had come under the authority of the Crown except Connecticut, Rhode Island, and two proprietary colonies, Maryland and Pennsylvania.

Whatever system of control existed, in charter colony, proprietary colony, or royal colony, they all had great opportunities for acquiring practice and experience in self-government. The laws passed by the legislative assemblies of the colonies had to be approved, either by some official authority in London or by the proprietor. But even when laws were disapproved, assemblies could alter the wording slightly and send a law back for approval, in the meantime operating under the law. The lapse of time was so great that colonial assemblies could sometimes stave off final disapproval of laws for a long period.

The religion of the thirteen colonies was diverse and was often the cause of dissension and political upheaval. The oldest colony, Virginia, had an Anglican establishment until the Revolution, as did South Carolina and New York. Although Maryland began as a refuge for Catholics, in 1702 the Church of England was also established there, and the later Calverts were Anglicans.

The best example of a theocratic state in the American colonies was of course the Massachusetts Bay in its early days. Although John Winthrop and the first Puritans professed to think of themselves as members of the Church of England seeking merely a place where they could practise their religion in its purity, they soon broke away from the established church to adopt a congregational form of church polity.

Implicit in Puritan doctrine, however, were motivations toward separatism, and the New England churches played an important part in the further colonization of New England. Under the leadership of their minister, a church congregation would emigrate to some region where they could be freer in the exercise of their religion. Several Connecticut towns were settled in this way. The first settlements in Rhode Island were established by discontented Puritans from Massachusetts Bay. Rhode Island, incidentally, was the one New England colony that emphasized toleration.

Pennsylvania was settled by a variety of religious groups seeking religious freedom. William Penn, himself a Quaker, saw to it that Quaker refugees found a welcome there, and indeed, for a long time Quakers were the controlling group in the colony. But Germans of many religious types came to Pennsylvania: Mennonites, quietists of various beliefs, and Lutherans. Presbyterians of Scottish extraction from Ulster also came in large numbers, as did Welsh Baptists. Pennsylvania welcomed religionists of all varieties. Even in colonies where a state church was nominally established, settlers of all kinds managed to find a place for themselves. Only in New England in the first few decades was religious conformity enforced with any degree of severity.

Education in the early days was a problem that troubled all of the colonies. In the more compact settlements of New England, schools could be maintained with greater effectiveness than in the agrarian colonies where plantations were far apart. But some effort was made everywhere to provide the rudiments of education. Soon after the establishment of Massachusetts Bay colony, Harvard College was founded in 1636 to ensure a supply of ministers, and, it was hoped, to provide education for Christian Indians, a dream that did not materialize. The College of William and Mary in Virginia was established in 1693 with some of the same objectives. William Penn and the Quakers of Philadelphia thought of education in more practical and more vocational terms.

The economic development of the colonies was slow at first because the founders did not know what they could produce and what would prove to be saleable commodities. From the beginning the colonies suffered from a shortage of labour. For that reason they welcomed indentured servants and at length accepted Negro slaves.

By chance, almost, John Rolfe in Virginia discovered that the sweet tobacco from the Caribbean or South America could be grown in

Virginia, and that commodity soon proved to be a source of wealth in the Chesapeake Bay colonies. Rice and indigo were profitably grown in South Carolina. Food grains, hogs, and cattle proved profitable in Pennsylvania and elsewhere. From the beginning, the fisheries and shipbuilding made New England prosperous, and the fur trade brought wealth to New York and to other colonies. The manufacture of rum from West Indian molasses proved to be another source of wealth for Massachusetts and Rhode Island. Rum became a medium of exchange in the slave trade on the west coast of Africa, and New Englanders grew rich from this trade.

The problem of the aborigines bothered the colonists from the beginning. According to the early charters, Englishmen had the right to take land not occupied by 'any Christian prince' as the phrase ran, and land held by the heathen could be appropriated at will. Fortunately for the earliest colonists, some devastating epidemic had swept through the Atlantic coastal tribes before the white man's arrival and had eliminated whole populations. In many areas, the first settlers found few Indians to dispute their possession. In other areas, especially in Pennsylvania, the settlers found it expedient to make treaties with the Indians and to purchase their lands.

But the relations between Indians and newcomers, with a few notable exceptions like Penn's series of treaties, were never very happy. Constant friction between the white man and the red resulted from the incursion of settlers into the Indians' hunting gounds. The wars between England and France during long periods in the eighteenth century involved their respective Indian allies. Greed for the wealth of the fur trade resulted in constant competition and friction. Finally, in 1763 the Crown sought to settle the problem of infiltration of settlers into the back country, which the Indians claimed as their hunting grounds, by establishing the Proclamation Line along the crest of the Allegheny Mountains. Beyond this line white settlers were forbiden to go. This gesture from London was as futile as King Canute's. Nothing could hold back the westward movement, and the Proclamation Line served merely as one more grievance of the colonists against the mother country.

Quarrels between Great Britain and the thirteen colonies rapidly developed after the Peace of Paris in 1763. The preceding wars had cost England vast sums, and it appeared to the government in London only just that the colonies should bear part of the expense of protecting them from French and Indian attacks. But British legislation was inept and tactless and colonial reaction was intemperate and violent. Soon quarrels developed into 'issues' and factionalism hardened into stubborn resistance. The passage of the Stamp Act, the Quartering Act, and other acts which the colonies interpreted as punitive measures at length brought on revolution.

The colonies were ill-prepared to resist Great Britain, for they had long resisted all efforts to unite them. William Penn, Benjamin Franklin, and others had urged plans of union which would have prepared the colonies for some concerted action, but all plans had failed. Not until the ineptitudes and the emotions of the decade from 1765 to 1775 could the colonies be brought into anything resembling a united body.

In the brief compass of a small book – at least one as small as this – one can reprint only a few highly selective documents representative of the development of aspects of the political and social life of the colonies that grew into the United States. Had space permitted, we could have presented a more comprehensive picture. We have tried, nevertheless, to select documents that suggest some of the main outlines of development.

I
COMPETING CLAIMS FOR THE NEW WORLD

1 Papal Bull concerning New Discoveries, May 4, 1493

The earliest rivals for territorial possessions beyond the seas were, by right of prime discovery, Portugal and Spain. At the time of Columbus' return from his first trans-Atlantic voyage, the reigning pope, Alexander VI, happened to be a Spaniard, of the Borgia line. On behalf of Ferdinand and Isabella, Alexander issued three successive papal bulls establishing their claim to sovereignty over the new-found territories beyond the western sea. The third of these, the bull *Inter caetera* of 4 May 1493, drew a line one hundred leagues west of any of the Azores or Cape Verde Islands and gave to Spain exclusive rights to territory, not in the possession of any other Christian prince, west of the line. Portugal was not mentioned by name.

It was this bull that subsequently evoked the wry comment from Francis I of France that he would like to see the will of his grandfather Adam to know by what right Spain claimed a patrimony of the whole of the New World.

Alexander, bishop, servant of the servants of God, to the illustrious sovereigns, our very dear son in Christ, Ferdinand, King, and our very dear daughter in Christ, Isabella, Queen, of Castile, Leon, Aragon, Sicily, and Granada, health and apostolic benediction. . . .

We have indeed learned that you, who for a long time had intended to seek out and discover certain islands and mainlands remote and unknown and not hitherto discovered by others . . . having been up to the present time greatly engaged in the siege and recovery of the kingdom itself of Granada, were unable to accomplish this holy and praiseworthy purpose. But, the said kingdom having at length been regained, as was pleasing to the Lord, you, with the wish to fulfill your desire, chose our beloved son, Christopher Columbus . . . whom you furnished with ships and men equipped for like designs. . . . And they at length, with divine aid and with the utmost diligence sailing in the ocean sea, discovered certain very remote islands and even mainlands that hitherto had not been discovered by others; wherein dwell very many peoples living in peace, and, as reported, going unclothed and not eating any flesh. . . .

In the islands and countries already discovered are found gold, spices, and very many other precious things of divers kinds and qualities. Wherefore, as becomes Catholic kings and princes . . . you have purposed with the favor of divine clemency to bring under your sway the said mainlands and islands. . . . We, of our own accord, not at your instance nor the request of anyone else in your regard, but of our own sole largess and certain knowledge and out of the fullness of our apostolic power . . . do by tenor of these presents . . . give, grant, and assign to you and your heirs and successors, kings of Castile and Leon, forever . . . all islands and mainlands found and to be found . . . towards the west and south, by drawing and establishing a line from the Arctic pole, namely the north, to the Antarctic pole, namely the south, no matter whether the said mainlands and islands are found and to be found in the direction of India or towards any other quarter, the said line to be distant one hundred leagues towards the west and south from any of the islands commonly known as the Azores and Cape Verde. With this proviso however that none of the islands and mainlands, found and to be found . . . beyond that said line towards the west and south, be in the actual possession of any Christian king or prince up to the birthday of our Lord Jesus Christ just past, from which the present year one thousand four hundred and ninety-three begins. . . .

Furthermore, under penalty of excommunication . . . we strictly forbid all persons of whatsoever rank, even imperial and royal, to dare, without your special permit or that of your aforesaid heirs and successors, to go for the purpose of trade or any other reason to the island or mainlands, found and to be found, towards the west and south . . . other decrees whatsoever to the contrary notwithstanding. . . .

Let no one, therefore, infringe, or with rash boldness contravene, this our recommendation, . . . mandate, prohibition, and will. Should anyone presume to attempt this, be it known to him that he will incur the wrath of Almighty God and of the blessed apostles Peter and Paul. Given at Rome, at St. Peter's, in the year of the incarnation of our Lord

one thousand four hundred and ninety-three, the fourth of May, and
the first year of our pontificate.

Gratis by order of our most holy lord, the Pope. . . .

Translation in *European Treaties Bearing on the
History of the United States and Its Dependencies
to 1648*, ed. F. G. Davenport (1917), pp. 75-8

2   Treaty of Tordesillas between Spain and Portugal, 1494

Portugal was unhappy about the division of the world by Pope Alexander VI.
Accordingly, after much negotiation, Spain and Portugal concluded a treaty
at Tordesillas on 7 June 1494, which moved the dividing line to 370 degrees
west of the Cape Verde Islands, thus establishing Portugal's claim to Brazil.
Since neither Spain nor Portugal knew how to determine the meridian precisely and could not agree on the number of leagues in a degree, the interpretation of the treaty long remained a matter of dispute.

Don Ferdinand and Doña Isabella, by the grace of God King and Queen
of Castile, Leon, Aragon, Sicily, Granada . . . by . . . members of our
council it was treated, adjusted, and agreed for us and in our name . . .
with the most serene Dom John, by the grace of God King of Portugal
and of the Algarves on this side and beyond the sea in Africa, Lord of
Guinea, our very dear and very beloved brother . . . as follows:

That, whereas a certain controversy exists between the said lords . . .
as to what lands, of all those discovered in the ocean sea up to the present day, the date of this treaty, pertain to each one of the said parts
respectively . . . their said representatives . . . covenanted and agreed
that a boundary or straight line be determined and drawn north and
south, from pole to pole, on the said ocean sea, from the Arctic to the
Antarctic pole. This boundary of line shall be drawn straight, as aforesaid, at a distance of three hundred and seventy leagues west of the
Cape Verde Islands, being calculated by degrees. . . . And all lands,
both islands and mainlands, found and discovered already, or to be
found and discovered hereafter, by the said King of Portugal and by
his vessels on this side of the said line and bound determined as above,
toward the east, in either north or south latitude, on the eastern side of
the said bound . . . shall belong to, and remain in the possession of, and
pertain forever to the said King of Portugal and his successors. And all
other lands, both islands and mainlands, found or to be found here-

after, discovered or to be discovered ... by the said King and Queen of Castile, Aragon, etc. and by their vessels, on the western side of the said bound ... shall belong to and remain in the possession of and pertain forever to the said King and Queen. ...

Item, ... from this date no ships shall be dispatched ... [of] the said King and Queen of Castile ... on this side the said bound, which pertains to the said King of Portugal and the Algarves, etc.; nor the said King of Portugal to the other part of the said bound, which pertains to the said King and Queen of Castile ... for the purpose of discovering and seeking any mainlands or islands, or for the purpose of trade, barter, or conquest of any kind.

Item, in order that the said line or bound of the said division may be made straight and as nearly as possible the said distance of three hundred and seventy leagues west of the Cape Verde Islands, ... within the ten months immediately following the date of this treaty their said constituent lords shall dispatch two or four caravels, namely, one or two by each one of them. ... These vessels shall meet at the Grand Canary Island during this time, and each one of the said parties shall send certain persons in them, to wit: pilots, astrologers, sailors, and any others they may deem desirable. But there must be as many on one side as on the other, and certain of the said pilots, astrologers, sailors, and others of those sent by the said King and Queen of Castile, Aragon, etc., and who are experienced, shall embark in the ships of the said King of Portugal and the Algarves; in like manner certain of the said persons sent by the said King of Portugal shall embark in the ship or ships of the said King and Queen of Castile. ...

European Treaties, ed. Davenport, pp. 93-6

3   English Letters patent to John Cabot, 1496

King Henry VII of England was interested in overseas exploration for the sake of trade. In view of the existing Spanish and Portuguese monopolies, underwritten by the Pope, he dared not venture into their known preserves. He therefore employed one Giovanni Caboto, 'another Genoese like Columbus' (naturalized as a citizen of Venice), to voyage in 'the eastern, western and northern sea', being careful to avoid the southern routes but otherwise disregarding, within two years, the Line of Demarcation.

The King, to all to whom, etc., greeting: Be it known that we have given and granted ... to our well-beloved John Cabot, citizen of Venice, to Lewis, Sebastian, and Santius, sons of the said John, and to the heirs of them . . . authority, leave, and power to sail to all parts, countries, and seas of the East, of the West, and of the North, under our banners and ensigns, with five ships . . . upon their own proper costs and charges, to seek out, discover, and find whatsoever isles, countries, regions, or provinces of the heathen and infidels . . . in what part of the world soever they be, which before this time have been unknown to all Christians. We have granted to them . . . licence to set up our banners and ensigns in every village, town, castle, isle, or mainland of them newly found. And that the aforesaid John and his sons, or their heirs and assigns, may subdue, occupy, and possess all such towns, cities, castles, and isles of them found . . . as our vassals and lieutenants, getting unto us the rule, title, and jurisdiction of the same. . . . The aforesaid John and his sons and heirs . . . be holden & bounden for every their voyage . . . to pay unto us, in wares or money, the fifth part of the capital gain so gotten; we giving & granting unto them and to their heirs and deputies that they shall be free from all paying of customs of all and singular such merchandise as they shall bring with them from those places so newly found.

And moreover we have given and granted to them . . . that all . . . places whatsoever they be that they shall chance to find . . . may not of any other of our subjects be frequented or visited without the licence of the foresaid John and his sons and their deputies, under pain of forfeiture as well of their ships, as of all and singular goods of all them that shall presume to sail to those places. . . .

Witness ourself at Westminster, the fifth day of March in the eleventh year of our reign.

By the King himself, etc.
From Richard Hakluyt, *Principal Navigations* (1589), pp. 510-11. Reprinted, with a different translation, in *The Precursors of Jacques Cartier, 1497-1534,* ed. H. P. Biggar (1911), pp. 8-10

4   Cabot Stakes an English Claim in North America, 1497

Contemporary reports of Cabot's successful voyage have survived in four letters. The first was written 23 August 1497 by Lorenzo Pasqualigo, a Venetian merchant, from London to his brothers in Venice.

The Venetian, our countryman, who went with a ship from Bristol in quest of new islands, is returned, and says that 700 leagues hence he discovered land, the territory of the Grand Cham (*Gram Cam*). He coasted for 300 leagues and landed; saw no human beings, but he has brought hither to the King certain snares which had been set to catch game, and a needle for making nets. He also found some felled trees, wherefore he supposed there were inhabitants, and returned to his ship in alarm.

He was three months on the voyage, and on his return he saw two islands to starboard, but would not land, time being precious, as he was short of provisions. He says that the tides are slack and do not flow as they do here. The King of England is much pleased with this intelligence.

The King has promised that in the spring our countryman shall have ten ships, armed to his order, and at his request has conceded him all prisoners, except such as are confined for high treason, to man his fleet. The King has also given him money wherewith to amuse himself till then, and he is now at Bristol with his wife, who is also Venetian, and with his sons. His name is Zuan Cabot, and he is styled the great admiral. Vast honor is paid him. He dresses in silk, and these English run after him like mad people, so that he can enlist as many of them as he pleases, and a number of our own rogues besides.

The discoverer of these places planted on his new-found land a large cross, with one flag of England and another of S. Mark, by reason of his being a Venetian, so that our banner has floated very far afield.

Calendar State Papers, Venice, I (1864), no. 752

5   London to Become a Great Mart for Spices

On 18 December 1497 a report of the Cabot voyage was written to Ludovico Sforza, Duke of Milan, by his ambassador in London. This letter is important for the light it casts upon the motives of both Cabot and Henry VII, as well as of the writer.

Perhaps amid the numerous occupations of your Excellency it may not weary you to hear how his Majesty here has gained a part of Asia, without a stroke of the sword. There is in this kingdom a man of the people, a Venetian, Messer Zoane Caboto by name, of kindly wit and a most expert mariner. Having observed that the sovereigns first of Portugal and then of Spain had occupied unknown islands, he decided to make a similar acquisition for his Majesty. After obtaining patents that the effective ownership of what he might find should be his, though reserving the rights of the Crown, he committed himself to Fortune in a little ship, with eighteen persons. He started from Bristol, a port on the west of this kingdom, passed Ireland, which is still further west, and then bore towards the north, in order to sail to the east, leaving the north on his right hand after some days. After having wandered for some time he at length arrived at the mainland, where he hoisted the royal standard and took possession for the king here. . . .

This Messer Zoane, as a foreigner and a poor man, would not have obtained credence had it not been that his companions, who are practically all English and from Bristol, testified that he spoke the truth. . . .

These same English, his companions, say that they could bring so many fish that this kingdom would have no further need of Iceland, from which place there comes a very great quantity of the fish called stockfish. But Messer Zoane has his mind set upon even greater things, because he proposes to keep along the coast from the place at which he touched, more and more towards the east, until he reaches an island which he calls Japan, situated in the equinoctial region, where he believes that all the spices in the world have their origin, as well as the jewels. . . .

He tells all this in such a way, and makes everything so plain, that I also feel compelled to believe him. What is much more, his Majesty, who is wise and not prodigal, also gives him some credence, because he is giving him a fairly good provision, since his return, so Messer Zoane himself tells me. Before very long they say that his Majesty will equip some ships, and in addition he will give them all the malefactors, and they will go to that country and form a colony. By means of this they hope to make London a more important mart for spices than Alexandria. . . .

I have also spoken with a Burgundian, one of Messer Zoane's companions, who corroborates everything. He wants to go back because the Admiral, which is the name they give to Messer Zoane, has given him an island. He has given another to his barber, a Genoese by birth, and both consider themselves counts, while my lord the Admiral esteems himself at least a prince.

I also believe that some poor Italian friars will go on this voyage, who have the promise of bishoprics. As I have made friends with the Admiral, I might have an archbishopric if I chose to go there, but I have reflected that the benefices which your Excellency reserves for me are safer, and I therefore beg that possession may be given me of those which fall vacant in my absence, and the necessary steps taken so that they may not be taken away from me by others, who have the advantage of being on the spot. Meanwhile I stay on in this country, eating ten or twelve courses at each meal, and spending three hours at table twice every day, for the love of your Excellency, to whom I humbly commend myself.

Cal. S.P., Milan, I (1912), no. 552

6   Cabot Has Encroached on the Spanish Domain, 1498

On 25 July 1498 Pedro de Ayala, a Spanish agent attached to the English court, included in a long intelligence report to his sovereigns such news of Cabot's voyages as he had been able to gather. In his opinion the English claim to the 'New-found land' was in violation of the Treaty of Tordesillas.

. . . I think your Majesties have already heard that the King of England has equipped a fleet in order to discover certain islands and mainland which he was informed some people from Bristol, who manned a few ships for the same purpose last year, had found. I have seen the map which the discoverer has made, who is another Genoese like Columbus. . . .

I, having seen the route which they took, and the distance they sailed, find that what they have found, or what they are in search of, is what your Highnesses already possess since it is, in fine, what fell to your Highnesses by the treaty with Portugal. . . . The King of England has often spoken to me on this subject. He hoped to derive great advantage from it. I think it is not further distant than four hundred leagues. I told him that, in my opinion, the land was already in the possession of your Majesties; but, though I gave him my reasons, he did not like it.

The Northmen, Columbus, and Cabot, 985–1503, ed. Edward G. Bourne [1906], pp. 429–30

7   Dr. John Dee Lists English Claims in North America, 1578

Dr. John Dee was a mathematician and astrologer who did much to advance English navigation in the later Tudor era. He provided the scientific nucleus for a group of expansionists and mariners that included Richard Chancellor, who opened the north-east route to Moscow for the Muscovy Company, Martin Frobisher, who sought the Northwest Passage, and Walter Raleigh, whose Roanoke colony was the first attempted by England. The following capitulation of English claims was drawn up by Dee in 1578.

A brief remembrance of sundry foreign regions discovered, inhabited and partly conquered by the subjects of this British monarchy: and so the lawful title of our Sovereign Lady Queen Elizabeth for the due claim and just recovery of the same disclosed. Which (in effect) is a Title Royal to all coasts and islands beginning at or about Terra Florida, alongst or near unto Atlantis, going northerly, and then to all the most northern islands, great and small, and so, compassing about Greenland until the territory opposite, unto the farthest easterly and northern bounds of the Duke of Muscovia his dominions; which last bounds are from our Albion more than half the sea voyage to the Cathayan westerly and northern sea coasts, as most evidently and at large it is declared in the volume of famous and rich discoveries.

Circa An. 1170. 1. The Lord Madoc, son to Owen Gwynedd, Prince of North Wales, led a colony and inhabited in Terra Florida or thereabouts.

Circa An. 1494. 2. Mr. Robert Thorn his father, and Mr. Eliot of Bristol, discovered Newfound Land.

Circa An. 560. 3. Brandan, the learned man, discovered very much of the western parts, but chiefly islands, unto one of which he gave the name Brandan, his island. And so is called at this present.

Circa An. 1497. 4. Sebastian Caboto [son of John, subsequently director of the Muscovy Company and friend of Dee], sent by King Henry the seventh, did discover from Newfound Land so far along and about the coast next to Labrador till he came to the latitude of 67½. And still found the seas open before him.

Anno 1576 et 1577. 5. The islands and broken land easterly and somewhat to the south of Labrador were more particularly discovered and possessed A° 1576 and the last year by Martin Frobisher, Esquire, and presently is by our people to be inhabited. The total content of which islands and parcel of land thereabout by our Sovereign Queen Elizabeth is lately named Meta Incognita.

Brit. Mus. Cotton MS. Aug. I.i.1. [1578]. Printed in *The Cabot Voyages and Bristol Discovery under Henry VII*, ed. J. A. Williamson (Hakluyt Soc., 1962), pp. 201-2.

II

MOTIVES AND PROPAGANDA FOR COLONIZATION

1 How Her Majesty May Annoy the King of Spain and Prevent a Mischief Betimes, 1577

On 6 November 1577 Dr. John Dee noted in his diary that 'Sir Humphrey Gilbert came to me to Mortlake'. Gilbert, an elder half-brother of Walter Raleigh, was a soldier and navigator who was among the first to pursue the idea of colonization in the New World. On the day of his visit to Dr. Dee, Gilbert addressed to Queen Elizabeth the memorandum that follows. Nine days later Francis Drake departed Plymouth on his voyage of circumnavigation, 'giving out his pretended voyage for Alexandria'.

A discourse how Her Majesty may annoy the King of Spain.

. . . The safety of principates, monarchies, and commonwealths rest[s] chiefly on making their enemies weak and poor, and themselves strong and rich, both which God hath specially wrought for Your Majesty's safety, if Your Highness shall not overpass good opportunities for the same when they are offered. . . .

First, Your Highness ought undoubtedly to seek the kingdom of heaven and, upon that foundation, to believe that there can never be constant and firm league of amity between those princes whose division is planted by the worm of their conscience. So that their leagues and fair words ought to be held but as mermaids' songs. . . . Which done, Your Majesty is to think that it is more than time to pare their nails by the stumps that are most ready prest to pluck the crown . . . from Your Highness's head. . . . Then, to foresee by all diligent means that your suspected neighbours may not have opportunity to recover breath whereby to repair their decayed losses; which, for your safety, is principally to be done by the farther weakening of their navies and by preserving and increasing of your own.

And the diminishing of their forces by sea is to be done either by open hostility or by some colourable means: as by giving of license under letters patents to discover and inhabit some strange place, with special proviso for their safeties whom policy requireth to have most annoyed. By which means the doing of the contrary shall be imputed to the executors' fault, Your Highness's letters patents being a manifest show that it was not Your Majesty's pleasure so to have it. After the public notice of which, in fact, Your Majesty is either to avow the same . . . or to disavow both them and the fact as league .breakers, leaving them to pretend it as done without your privity. . . .

This cloak being had for the reign, the way to work the feat is to set forth under such like colour of discovery certain ships of war to the N.L. [New Land] which, with your good license, I will undertake without Your Majesty's charge. In which place they shall certainly once in the year meet in effect all the great shipping of France, Spain, and Portugal; where I would have take and bring away with these freights and ladings the best of those ships and to burn the worst. And those that they take, to carry into Holland or Zeeland or, as pirates, to shroud themselves for a small time upon Your Majesty's coasts under the friendship of some certain vice-admiral of this realm; who may be afterwards committed to prison, as in displeasure for the same. . . .

The setting forth of shipping for this service will amount to no great matter, and the return shall certainly be with great gain. For the N.F. [Newland Fish] is a principal and rich and everywhere vendible merchandise. And by the gain thereof shipping, victual, munition, and the transporting of five or six thousand soldiers may be defrayed.

It may be said that a few ships cannot possibly distress so many. And that, although by this service you take or destroy all the shipping you find of theirs in those places, yet are they but subjects' ships, their own particular navies being nothing lessened thereby, and therefore their forces shall not so much be diminished as it is supposed, whereunto I answer:

There is no doubt to perform it without danger. For although they may be many in number, and great of burden, yet they are furnished with men – and munition – but like fishers. And when they come upon the coasts they do always disperse themselves into sundry ports, and do disbark the most of their people into small boats for the taking and drying of their fish, leaving few or none aboard their ships, so that there is as little doubt of the easy taking and carrying of them away as of the decaying hereby of those princes' forces by sea. For their own proper shippings are very few, and of small forces in respect of the others; and their subjects' shipping, being once destroyed, it is likely that they will never be repaired, partly through the decay of the owners and partly through the losses of the trades whereby they maintained the same. . . . But if they should, it will require a long time to season timber for that purpose. . . .

It may also be objected that although this may be done in act, yet is it not allowable, being against Your Majesty's league. For although by the reach of reason men's eyes may be obscured, yet unto God nothing is hidden, which I answer thus:

I hold it as lawful in Christian policy to prevent a mischief betimes as to revenge it too late, especially seeing that God Himself is a party in the common quarrels now afoot, and His enemy['s] malicious disposition towards Your Highness and His Church manifestly seen, although by God's merciful providence not yet thoroughly felt.

Further it may be said that if this should be done by Englishmen under what colour soever they should shroud themselves, yet will that cut us off from all traffic with those that shall be annoyed by such means, and thereby utterly undo the state of merchandise, decay the maintenance of the shipping of this realm, and also greatly diminish Your Majesty's customs. To which I reply thus:

. . . The forces of the Spaniards and Portuguese being there so much decayed as aforesaid, the French of necessity shall be brought under Your Highness's lie. Assuring Your Majesty, the case being as it is, it were better a thousand fold thus to gain the start of them rather than yearly to submit ourselves subject to have all the merchants' ships of this realm stayed in their hands, whereby they shall be armed at our costs to beat us with rods of our own making. . . .

If Your Highness will permit me with my associates either overtly or covertly to perform the aforesaid enterprise, then with the gain thereof there may be easily such a competent company transported to the W.I. [West Indies] as may be able not only to dispossess the S. [Spaniards] thereof, but also to possess forever Your Majesty and realm therewith. . . . By which means Your Highness's doubtful friends, or rather apparent enemies, shall not be only made weak and poor, but therewith yourself and realm made strong and rich, both by sea and by land, as well there as here. . . . Then of force this realm, being an island, shall be discharged from all foreign perils if all the monarchies of the world should join against us – so long as Ireland shall be in safe-keeping, the league of Scotland maintained, and further amity concluded with the Prince of Orange and the King of Denmark. By which means also Your Majesty shall engraft and glue to your crown, in effect, all the northern and southern voyages of the world, so that none shall be then well able to cross the seas but subject to Your Highness's devotion, considering the great increase of shipping that will grow and be maintained by those long voyages. . . .

And if I may perceive that Your Highness shall like of this enterprise, then will I most willingly express my simple opinion which way the W.I. may without difficulty be more surprised and defended. . . . But if Your Majesty like to do it at all, then would I wish Your Highness to consider that delay doth often times prevent the performance of good things. For the wings of man's life are plumed with the feathers of death.

. . . November 6, 1577.

> You Majesty's most faithful servant and subject.
>
> H. Gilbert
>
> P.R.O., S.P. Dom., Eliz. 12/118, 12. Printed in W. G. Gosling, *The Life of Sir Humphrey Gilbert* (1911), pp. 133-39

2   Newfoundland Annexed for England, 1583

In 1578 Sir Humphrey Gilbert was granted a patent, valid for six years, 'to search, find out, and view such remote, heathen, and barbarous lands . . . not actually possessed of any Christian prince'. Despite his sanguine assurance to the Queen that there was 'no doubt to perform it without danger', Gilbert's first expedition was a failure. On the ill-fated voyage of 1583, he reached Newfoundland where, on August 5, he sailed into St. John's harbour and formally took possession of the land in the name of Queen Elizabeth. Gilbert is perhaps equally remembered for the bold gesture with which he met death on the homeward passage.

A report of the voyage and success thereof attempted in the year of our Lord 1583 by Sir Humphrey Gilbert, Knight, with other gentlemen assisting him in that action, intended to discover and to plant Christian inhabitants in place convenient . . . not in the actual possession of any Christian prince. . . .

The first discovery of these coasts (never heard of before) was well begun by John Cabot, the father, and Sebastian his son, an Englishman born, who were the first finders-out of all that great tract of land stretching from the cape of Florida unto those islands which we now call the Newfoundland. All which they brought and annexed unto the Crown of England....

Seeing the English nation only hath right unto these countries of America, from the cape of Florida northward, by the privilege of first discovery, unto which Cabot was authorized by regal authority and set forth by the expense of our late famous king, Henry VII; which right also seemeth strongly defended on our behalf by the powerful hand of almighty God, withstanding the enterprises of other nations: it may greatly encourage us, upon so just ground ... to prosecute effectually unto a full possession of those so ample and pleasant countries....

From Saturday, the 15 of June, until the 28, which was upon a Friday, we never had fair day without fog or rain, and winds bad, much to the west northwest, whereby we were driven southward to 41 degrees scarce.

About this time of the year the winds are commonly west towards the Newfound land, keeping ordinarily within two points of west to the south or to the north, whereby the course thither falleth out to be long and tedious after June which in March, April, and May hath been performed out of England in 22 days and less. We had wind always so scant from west northwest, and from west southwest again, that our traverse was great, running south unto 41 degrees almost, and afterward north into 51 degrees....

Forsaking this bay and uncomfortable coast (nothing appearing unto us but hideous rocks and mountains, bare of trees and void of any green herb), we followed the coast to the south, with weather fair and clear ... until we came against the harbour called St. John's, about 5 leagues from the former cape of St. Francis where, before the entrance into the harbour, we found also the frigate, or *Squirrel*, lying at anchor....

Having taken place convenient in the road, we let fall anchors, the captains and masters repairing aboard our admiral [flagship]. Whither also came immediately the masters and owners of the fishing fleet of Englishmen to understand the General's intent and cause of our arrival there. They were all satisfied when the General had showed his commission and purpose to take possession of those lands to the behalf of the Crown of England and the advancement of Christian religion in those paganish regions, requiring but their lawful aid for repairing of his fleet and supply of some necessaries....

Monday following, the General had his tent set up, who, being accompanied with his own followers, summoned the merchants and masters, both English and strangers, to be present at his taking possession of those countries. Before whom openly was read and interpreted unto the strangers his commission, by virtue whereof he took posses-sion in the same harbour of St. John's and 200 leagues every way; in-vested the Queen's Majesty with the title and dignity thereof; had de-livered unto him (after the custom of England) a rod and a turf of the same soil, entering possession also for him, his heirs and assigns forever. And signified unto all men that, from that time forward, they should take the same land as a territory appertaining to the Queen of England, and himself authorized under Her Majesty to possess and enjoy it and to ordain laws for the government thereof agreeable (so near as con-veniently might be) unto the laws of England. Under which all people coming thither hereafter, either to inhabit or by way of traffic, should be subjected and governed. . . .

Monday the ninth of September, in the afternoon, the frigate was near cast away, oppressed by waves, yet at that time recovered. And giving forth signs of joy the General, sitting abaft with a book in his hand, cried out unto us in the *Hind* (so oft as we did approach within hearing), 'We are as near to heaven by sea as by land!' Reiterating the same speech, well beseeming a soldier resolute in Jesus Christ, as I can testify he was.

The same Monday night, about twelve of the clock or not long after, the frigate being ahead of us in the *Golden Hind*, suddenly her lights were out whereof, as it were in a moment, we lost the sight; and withal our watch cried the General was cast away, which was too true. For in that moment the frigate was devoured and swallowed up of the sea.

Hakluyt, *Principal Navigations* (1589), pp. 679-95. Reprinted in *Voyages and Colonising Enterprises of Sir Humphrey Gilbert*, ed. D. B. Quinn (Hak. Soc., 1940), ii.385-420

3   Hakluyt States the Case for Colonies, 1584

Richard Hakluyt, compiler and editor of *The Principal Navigations . . . of the English Nation* (1589; expanded ed., 1598-1600) was associated with the circle of expansionists that included Dr. Dee, Gilbert, Raleigh, Walsingham, and, among others, his elder cousin, Richard Hakluyt the lawyer. The younger Hakluyt was a clergyman and geographer. Upon the lapse of Gilbert's patent in 1584, Raleigh secured a new patent for himself and sent out two ships to reconnoitre the North American coast. At his behest, Hakluyt wrote the tract generally known as *The Discourse of Western Planting* for the purpose of winning the support of the Queen, who received it from Hakluyt's hand on 5 October 1584. Closely guarded at the time, the document was not published until 1877.

A particular discourse concerning the great necessity and manifold commodities that are like to grow to this realm of England by the western discoveries lately attempted. Written in the year 1584 by Richard Hakluyt of Oxford at the request and direction of the right worshipful Mr. Walter Raleigh, now Knight, before the coming home of his two barks. . . .

Chapter 20
[Recapitulation of the arguments]

A brief collection of certain reasons to induce Her Majesty and the state to take in hand the western voyage and the planting there.

1. The soil yieldeth and may be made to yield all the several commodities of Europe, and of all kingdoms, dominions, and territories that England tradeth with, that by trade of merchandise cometh into this realm.

2. The passage thither and home is neither too long nor too short but easy, and to be made twice in the year.

3. The passage cutteth not near the trade of any prince, nor near any of their countries or territories, and is a safe passage and not easy to be annoyed by prince or potentate whatsoever.

4. The passage is to be performed at all times of the year, and in that respect passeth our trades in the Levant seas within the Straits of Gibraltar, and the trades in the seas within the King of Denmark's strait, and the trades to the ports of Norway and of Russia, etc. . . .

5. And where England now for certain hundred years last past, by the peculiar commodity of wools, and of later years by clothing of the same, hath raised itself from meaner state to greater wealth and much higher honour, might, and power than before . . .: it cometh now so to pass that, by the great endeavour of the increase of the trade of wools in Spain and in the West Indies . . . the wools of England and the cloth made of the same will become base [debased in value] and every day more base than other; which prudently weighed, it behooveth this realm . . . to foresee and to plant at Norumbega or some like place, were it not for any thing else but for the hope of the vent of our wool indraped. . . . And, effectually pursuing that course, we shall not only find on that tract of land . . . (to whom warm cloth shall be right welcome), an ample vent, but also shall . . . find out known and unknown islands and dominions replenished with people that may fully

vent the abundance of that our commodity that else will in few years wax of none or of small value by foreign abundance, etc. . . . The increase of the wools of Spain and America is of high policy, with great desire of our overthrow endeavoured; and the goodness of the foreign wools our people will not enter into the consideration of, nor will not believe aught, they be so sotted with opinion of their own; and if it be not foreseen and some such place of vent provided, farewell the good state of all degrees in this realm.

6. This enterprise may stay the Spanish king from flowing over all the face of that waste firm [continent] of America, if we seat and plant there in time. . . . There is no comparison between the ports of the coasts that the King of Spain doth now possess and use and the ports of the coasts that our nation is to possess by planting at Norumbega and on that tract fast by, more to the North and North-east; and . . . there is from thence a much shorter course, and a course of more temperature, and a course that possesseth more continuance of ordinary winds, than the present course of the Spanish Indian navy's now doth. And England possessing the purposed place of planting, Her Majesty may, by the benefit of the seat having won good and royal havens, have plenty of excellent trees for masts, of goodly timber to build ships and to make great navies, of pitch, tar, hemp, and all things incident for a navy royal, and that for no price and without money or request. How easy a matter may it be to this realm, swarming at this day with valiant youths rusting and hurtful by lack of employment, and having good makers of cable and of all sorts of cordage, and the best and most cunning shipwrights of the world, to be lords of all those seas, and to spoil Philip's Indian navy and to deprive him of yearly passage of his treasure into Europe, and consequently to abate the pride of Spain and of the supporter of the great Antichrist of Rome, and to pull him down in equality to his neighbour princes, and consequently to cut off the common mischiefs that come to all Europe by the peculiar abundance of his Indian treasure, and this without difficulty.

7. [The distance of the voyage will require large ships] . . . so as this realm shall have by that mean ships of great burden and of great strength for the defence of this realm and for the defence of that new seat, . . . and withal great increase of perfect seamen . . . which kind o men are neither nourished in few days nor in few years.

8. This new navy of mighty, new, strong ships . . . shall never be subject to arrest of any prince or potentate, as the navy of this realm

from time to time hath been in the ports of the Empire, in the ports of the Base Countries [Low Countries], in Spain, France, Portugal, etc. . . . and so always ready . . . to offend and defend as shall be required.

9. The great mass of wealth of the realm embarked in the merchants' ships carried out in this new course shall not lightly, in so far distant a course from the coast of Europe, be driven by winds and tempests into ports of any foreign princes, . . . and so our merchants . . . are by this voyage out of one great mischief.

10. No foreign commodity that comes into England comes without payment of custom once, twice, or thrice before it come into the realm, and so all foreign commodities become dearer to the subjects of this realm; and by this course to Norumbega foreign princes' customs are avoided and, the foreign commodities cheaply purchased, they become cheap to the subjects of England. . . .

11. At the first traffic with the people of those parts the subjects of this realm for many years shall change many cheap commodities of these parts for things of high valour [value] there not esteemed. . . .

12. By the great plenty of those regions the merchants and their factors shall lie there cheap, buy and repair their ships cheap, and shall return at pleasure without stay or restraint of foreign prince . . . and buying his wares cheap, may maintain trade with small stock and without taking up money upon interest. . . .

13. By making of ships and by preparing of things for the same . . . and by thousands of things there to be done, infinite numbers of the English nation may be set on work, to the unburdening of the realm with many that now live chargeable to the state at home.

14. If the sea-coast serve for making of salt, and the inland for wine, oils, oranges, lemons, figs, etc. . . . without sword drawn we shall cut the comb of the French, of the Spanish, of the Portingale, and of enemies and of doubtful friends. . . .

15. The substances serving, we may out of those parts receive the mass of wrought wares that now we receive out of France, Flanders, Germany, etc., and so we may daunt the pride of some enemies of this realm. . . .

16. We shall by planting there enlarge the glory of the Gospel and om England plant sincere religion, and provide a safe and sure place to receive people from all parts of the world that are forced to flee for the truth of God's Word.

17. If frontier wars there chance to arise, . . . it will occasion the training-up of our youth in the discipline of war. . . .

18. The Spaniards govern in the Indies with all pride and tyranny, and, like as when people of contrary nature at the sea enter into galleys, where men are tied as slaves, all yell and cry with one voice '*liberta, liberta*' . . . so no doubt whensoever the Queen of England, a prince of such clemency, shall seat upon that firm of America and shall be reported throughout all that tract to use the natural people there with all humanity, courtesy, and freedom, they will yield themselves to her government and revolt clean from the Spaniard, and specially when they shall understand that she hath a noble navy and that she aboundeth with a people most valiant for their defence. . . . And this brought so about, Her Majesty and her subjects may both enjoy the treasure of the mines of gold and silver, and the whole trade . . . of merchandise that now passeth thither by the Spaniards' only hand of all the commodities of Europe. . . .

19. The present short trades causeth the mariner to be cast off and oft to be idle, and so by poverty to fall to piracy; but this course to Norumbega, being longer and a continuance of the employment of the mariner, doth keep the mariner from idleness and from necessity, and so it cutteth off the principal actions of piracy, and the rather because no rich prey for them to take cometh directly in their course. . . .

20. Many men of excellent wits and of divers singular gifts, overthrown by suretyship, by sea, or by some folly of youth . . . may there . . . do their country good service; and . . . the saving of great numbers that for trifles may otherwise be devoured by the gallows.

21. Many soldiers . . . in the end of the wars . . . may there be unladen, to the common profit and quiet of this realm. . . .

22. The fry [children] of the wandering beggars of England . . . may there be unladen, better bred up, and may people waste countries, to the home and foreign benefit and to their own more happy state.

23. If England cry out and affrm that there is so many in all trades that one cannot live for another, as in all places they do, this Norumbega (if it be thought so good) offereth the remedy.

First printed as *A Discourse concerning Western Planting*, ed. Leonard Woods (*Collections of the Maine Historical Soc.*, 1877), pp. 152-61. Reprinted in *The Original Writings . . . of the Two Richard Hakluyts*, ed. E. G. R. Taylor (Hakluyt Soc., 1935), ii.313-19

4 'Spoil and Riches of Most Force with the Common Soldier'

As in all times, high policy in the age of colonization was beyond the ken of the common folk. Yet everyone shared a common motive for enterprise in the New World: the hope of quick riches. Few Elizabethans realized this more keenly than Walter Raleigh, as he makes clear in the following passage:

We find it in daily experience that all discourse of magnanimity, of national virtue, of religion, of liberty, and whatsoever else hath been wont to move and encourage virtuous men hath no force at all with the common soldier in comparison of spoil and riches. The rich ships are boarded upon all disadvantages, the rich towns are furiously assaulted, and the plentiful countries willingly invaded. Our English nations have attempted many places in the Indies, and run upon the Spaniards headlong, in hope of their rials of plate and pistolets which, had they been put to it upon the like disadvantages in Ireland, or in any poor country, they would have turned their pieces and pikes against their commanders, contesting that they had been brought without reason to the butchery and slaughter. It is true that the war is made willingly and, for the most part, with good success, that is ordained against the richest nations. For as the needy are always adventurous, so plenty is wont to shun peril; and men that have well to live do rather study how to live well, I mean wealthily, than care to die (as they call it) honourably. *Car où il n'y a rien à gaigner que des coups volontiers, il n'y va pas*: No man makes haste to the market where there is nothing to be bought but blows.

Sir Walter Raleigh, *History of the World* (1614), Bk. iv, chap. 2, p. 178. Reprinted in *The Roanoke Voyages*, ed. D. B. Quinn (Hak. Soc., 1955), i.223-4

5 England's Right to a Fair Land in the New World, 1609

After the planting of the colony at Jamestown (1607) by the Virginia Company of London, much of the propaganda for colonization was carried on by the joint-stock company and its subscribers. One of these wrote the tract *Nova Britannia* (1609) that reiterated England's right to most of the eastern seaboard of North America and summarized its inducements, real and imagined, for colonists. Despite the rivers 'abounding with store of fish', the winter of 1609-10 was known as the 'starving time' when the colony nearly perished.

... There are divers monuments already published in print to the world manifesting and showing that the coasts and parts of Virginia have been long since discovered, peopled, & possessed by many English, both men, women, and children, the natural subjects of our late Queen Elizabeth of famous memory, conducted and left there at sundry times; and that the same footing and possession is there yet kept and possessed by the same English or by their seed and offspring ... to this day. Which argueth sufficiently to us (and it is true) that over those English and Indian people no Christian king or prince (other than James our Sovereign Lord and King) ought to have rule or dominion, nor can by possession, conquest, or inheritance truly claim or make just title to those territories or to any part thereof, except it be (as we hear of late) that a challenge is laid to all by virtue of a donation from Alexander the Sixth, Pope of Rome, wherein (they say) is given all the West Indies, including Florida and Virginia, with all America and whatsoever islands adjacent.

But what is this to us? They are blind indeed that stumble here. It is much like that great Donation of Constantine whereby the Pope himself doth hold and claim the city of Rome and all the Western Empire, ... the whole West Empire from a temporal prince to the Pope, and the whole West Indies from the Pope to a temporal prince. I do verily guess they be near of kin, they are so like each other. ...

And now in describing the natural seat and disposition of the country itself: ... First, the voyage is not long nor tedious, six weeks at ease will send us thither, whereas six months suffice not to some other places where we trade. Our course and passage is through the great ocean, where is no fear of rocks or flats, nor subject to the straits and restraint of foreign princes; most winds that blow are apt and fit for us and none can hinder us; when we come at the coast there is continual depth enough, with good bottom for anchorhold, and the land is fair to fall withal, full of excellent good harbours. ...

Two goodly rivers are discovered winding far into the main, the one in the north part of the land by our western colony, knights and gentlemen of greater Plymouth and others; the other in the south part thereof by our colony of London: upon which river, being both broad, deep, and pleasant, abounding with store of fish, our colony have begun to fortify themselves and have built a town and named it (in honour of our king) Jamestown, fourscore miles within-land, upon the north side of the river (as is London upon the river of Thames), from whence we have discovered the same river one hundred miles further into the mainland. In the searching whereof they were so ravished with the admirable sweetness of the stream and with the pleasant land trending along on either side that their joy exceeded and with great admiration they praised God.

The country itself is large and great, assuredly, though as yet no exact discovery can be made of all; . . . the air and climate most sweet and wholesome, much warmer than England and very agreeable to our natures. It is inhabited with wild and savage people that live and lie up and down in troops, like herds of deer in a forest: they have no law but Nature, their apparel skins of beasts, but most go naked. . . . They are generally very loving and gentle and do entertain and relieve our people with great kindness. They are easy to be wrought good, and would fain embrace a better condition. The land yieldeth naturally for the sustentation of man abundance of fish, both scale and shell; of land- and water-fowls infinite store; of deer, rein and fallow; stags, conies, and hares; with many fruits and roots good for meat.

There are valleys and plains streaming with sweet springs, like veins in a natural body. There are hills and mountains, making a sensible proffer of hidden treasure never yet searched. The land is full of minerals; plenty of woods (the wants of England) are there growing . . . in great abundance. . . . It yieldeth also rosin, turpentine, pitch, and tar; sassafras, mulberry trees, and silkworms; many skins and rich furs; many sweet woods, and dyers' woods and other costly dyes; plenty of sturgeon; timber for shipping – mast, plank, and deal; soap-ashes; caviar; and what else we know not yet because our days are young. . . .

And as for our supplanting the savages, we have no such intent: our intrusion into their possessions shall tend to their great good and no way to their hurt, unless, as unbridled beasts, they procure it to them-selves. We propose to proclaim and make it known to them all, by some public interpretation, that our coming thither is to plant our-selves in their country, yet not to supplant and root them out but to bring them from their base condition to a far better. . . .

[Robert Johnson], *Nova Britannia. Offering Most Excellent Fruits by Planting in Virginia* (1609), facs. reprint for J. Sabin (1867), *passim*

6   Oglethorpe's Design for Establishing a Colony of Georgia, 1733

General James E. Oglethorpe, a Member of the English House of Commons, in the course of a distinguished military career won a reputation for executive ability and humanity. Appointed chairman of a committee to investigate and reform the prisons, he conceived the idea of founding a colony for worthy unfortunates who crowded debtors' prisons in England. His proposals, more realistic than many of his predecessors', were published, with a sermon by Samuel Smith, in 1733.

In America there are fertile lands sufficient to subsist all the useless poor in England and distressed Protestants in Europe, yet thousands starve for want of mere sustenance. The distance makes it difficult to get thither. The same want that renders men useless here prevents their paying their passage; and if others pay it for them they become servants, or rather slaves, for years to those who have defrayed the expense. Therefore, money for passage is necessary, but it is not the only want; for if people were set down in America, and the land before them, they must cut down trees, build houses, fortify towns, dig and sow the land before they can get in a harvest; and till then they must be provided with food and kept together, that they may be assistant to each other for their natural support and protection.

The Romans esteemed the sending forth of colonies among their noblest works. They observed that Rome, as she increased in power and empire, drew together such a conflux of people from all parts that she found herself overburdened with their number. . . . Necessity, the mother of invention, suggested to them an expedient which at once gave ease to the capital and increased the wealth and number of industrious citizens by lessening the useless and unruly multitude; and by planting them in colonies on the frontiers of their empire gave a new strength to the whole. And this they looked upon to be so considerable a service to the commonwealth that they created peculiar officers for the establishment of such colonies, and the expense was defrayed out of the public treasury. . . .

The colony of Georgia lying about the same latitude with part of China, Persia, Palestine, and the Madeiras, it is highly probable that, when hereafter it shall be well peopled and rightly cultivated, England may be supplied from thence with raw silk, wine, oil, dyes, drugs, and many other materials for manufactures which she is obliged to purchase from southern countries. As towns are established and grow populous along the rivers Savannah and Altamaha, they will make such a barrier as will render the southern frontier of the British colonies on the continent of America safe from Indian and other enemies. . . .

Christianity will be extended by the execution of this design, since the good discipline established by the society will reform the manners of those miserable objects who shall be by them subsisted, and the example of a whole colony, who shall behave in a just, moral, and religious manner, will contribute greatly towards the conversion of the Indians. . . .

The trustees in their general meetings will consider of the most prudent methods for effectually establishing a regular colony, and that it may be done is demonstrable. Under what difficulties was Virginia planted? The coast and climate then unknown, the Indians numerous and at enmity with the first planters, who were forced to fetch all provisions from England. Yet it is grown a mighty province and the revenue receives £100,000 for duties upon the goods that they send yearly home. . . .

This new colony is more likely to succeed than either of the former were, since Carolina abounds with provisions, the climate is known, and there are men to instruct in the seasons and nature of cultivating the soil. There are but few Indian families within 400 miles, and those in perfect amity with the English. . . . If the colony is attacked, it may be relieved by sea from Port Royal or the Bahamas, and the militia of South Carolina is ready to support it by land.

For the continuing the relief which is now given, there will be lands reserved in the colony, and the benefit arising from them is to go to the carrying on of the trust. . . .

There is an occasion now offered for everyone to help forward this design. The smallest benefaction will be received and applied with the utmost care. Every little will do something, and a great number of small benefactions will amount to a sum capable of doing a great deal of good. . . .

James Oglethorpe, *Some Account of the Designs of the Trustees for Establishing the Colony of Georgia in America* (1733). Reprinted in *American Colonial Documents to 1776* (*English Historical Documents*, IX), ed. Merrill Jensen (1955), pp. 128-31

III

CHARTERS, COMPACTS AND LAWS

1 Letters Patent to Walter Raleigh, 1584

Walter Raleigh had participated in both expeditions of his half-brother, Sir Humphrey Gilbert, to the New World. After Gilbert was lost at sea in 1583, Raleigh petitioned for his unexpired licence to explore and colonize. The two patents were almost identical, with the major exception that the Grand Banks fishery and Newfoundland, already annexed for the Crown by Gilbert, were excluded from Raleigh's jurisdiction.

The letters patents granted by the Queen's Majesty to M[aster] Walter Raleigh, now Knight, for the discovering and planting of new lands and countries, to continue the space and time of 6 years and no more.

Elizabeth, by the grace of God of England, France and Ireland Queen, defender of the faith, etc. To all people to whom these presents shall come, greeting. Know ye that of our especial grace, certain science, and mere motion we have given and granted and by these presents for us, our heirs and successors do give and grant to our trusty and well beloved servant Walter Raleigh, Esquire, and to his heirs and assigns forever free liberty and license from time to time and at all times forever hereafter to discover, search, find out, and view such remote, heathen, and barbarous lands, countries, and territories not actually possessed of any Christian prince nor inhabited by Christian people as to him, his heirs and assigns and to every or any of them shall seem good; and the same to have, hold, occupy, and enjoy to him, his heirs and assigns forever with all prerogatives . . ., both by sea and land, whatsoever we by our letters patents may grant and as we or any of our noble progenitors have heretofore granted to any person or persons, bodies politic or corporate.

And the said Walter Raleigh, his heirs and assigns and all such as . . . shall go or travel thither to inhabit or remain, there to build and fortify at the discretion of the said Walter Raleigh . . . the statutes or acts of

Parliament made against fugitives . . . or any ordinance whatsoever to the contrary in any wise notwithstanding.

And we do likewise by these presents . . . give and grant full authority, liberty and power to the said Walter Raleigh . . . that he . . . shall and may . . . have, take, and lead in the said voyage and travel thitherward, or to inhabit there with him . . . such and so many of our subjects as shall willingly accompany him . . . and also to have, take and employ, and use sufficient shipping and furniture for the transportations and navigations. . . .

And further that the said Walter Raleigh . . . shall have, hold, occupy, and enjoy . . . forever all the soil of all such lands . . . to be discovered and possessed as aforesaid, and of all such cities, castles, towns, villages, and places in the same with the rights . . . to be had or used with full power to dispose thereof and of every part in fee simple or otherwise according to the order of the laws of England . . . reserving always to us, our heirs and successors for all services, duties, and demands the first [sic! scribal error for fifth] part of all the ore of gold and silver that from time to time . . . after such discovery, subduing, and possessing shall be there gotten and obtained. All which lands, countries, and territories shall forever be holden of the said Walter Raleigh, his heirs and assigns of us, our heirs and successors by homage and by the said payment of the said fifth part reserved only for all services.

And moreover we do by these presents . . . grant license to the said Walter Raleigh . . . that he . . . shall and may . . . hereafter for his and their defence encounter and expulse, repel and resist, as well by sea as by land and by all other ways whatsoever, all and every such person and persons whatsoever as, without the especial liking and license of the said Walter Raleigh and of his heirs and assigns, shall attempt to inhabit within the said countries . . . (the subjects of our realms and dominions and all other persons in amity with us trading to the new found lands for fishing as heretofore they have commonly used, or being driven by force of a tempest or shipwreck, only excepted). . . .

And for uniting in more perfect league and amity of such countries . . . with our realms of England and Ireland, and the better encouragement of men to these enterprises, we do by these presents grant and declare that all such countries so hereafter to be possessed . . . from thenceforth shall be of the allegiance of us, our heirs and successors. And we do grant to the said Walter Raleigh, his heirs and assigns . . . that they and every or any of them being either born within our said realms of England or Ireland or in any other place within our allegiance . . . shall and may have all the privileges of free denizens and persons native of England. . . .

We . . . do give and grant to the said Walter Raleigh . . . that he . . . shall and may . . . have full and mere power and authority to correct, punish, pardon, govern and rule . . . all such our subjects as . . . shall at any time hereafter inhabit any such lands . . . according to such statutes, laws, and ordinances as shall be by him, the said Walter Raleigh . . . devised or established for the better government of the said people . . . so always as the said statutes . . . may be as near as conveniently may be agreeable to the form of the laws . . . or policy of England . . . nor in any wise to withdraw any of the subjects or people of those lands or places from the allegiance of us, our heirs and successors as their immediate sovereign under God. . . .

Provided always . . . that if the said Walter Raleigh . . . shall at any time or times hereafter rob or spoil by sea or by land, or do any act of unjust or unlawful hostility to any the subjects of us, our heirs or successors, or to any of the subjects of any the kings . . . or estates being then in perfect league and amity with us, our heirs and successors; that upon such injury, or upon just complaint of any such prince . . . we . . . shall make open proclamation within any the ports of our realm of England that the said Walter Raleigh, . . . and assigns and adherents or any to whom these our letters patents may extend, shall, within the terms to be limited by such proclamation, make full restitution and satisfaction of all such injuries done so as both we and the said princes or other so complaining may hold us and themselves fully contented. And that if the said Walter Raleigh . . . shall not make or cause to be made satisfaction accordingly, within such time so to be limited, that then it shall be lawful to us . . . to put the said Walter Raleigh . . . and all the inhabitants of the said places to be discovered (as is aforesaid) or any of them, out of our allegiance and protection. And that from and after such time of putting out of protection of the said Walter Raleigh . . . the said places . . . shall be out of our allegiance and protection and free for all princes and others to pursue with hostility, as being not our subjects nor by us any way to be avouched, maintained, or defended . . . any other grant . . . to the contrary thereof, before this time given . . . in any wise notwithstanding.

In witness whereof we have caused these our letters to be made patents. Witness ourselves at Westminster the 25. day of March in the six and twentieth year of our reign.

Hakluyt, *Principal Navigations* (1589), pp. 725-8.
Reprinted, *Roanoke Voyages*, ed. Quinn, i.82-9

2   Third Charter of the Virginia Company, 1612

The first charters issued for colonization followed the type of charter issued to joint stock companies, which gave them the right to engage in trade and to establish ordinances and laws governing their establishments. The first charter granted by King James I to the Virginia Company in 1606, however, introduced a new factor, that of the royal prerogative in certain appointments, notably a council appointed by the King, to have its headquarters in London. Neither this charter nor the second charter proved satisfactory. In 1612, King James issued a third charter which was followed fairly closely by Charles I in issuing a charter to the Massachusetts Bay Company in 1629.

James, by the grace of God, king of England, Scotland, France, and Ireland, defender of the faith. . . . Whereas, at the humble suit of divers and sundry our loving subjects, as well adventurers as planters of the first colony in Virginia, and for the propagation of Christian religion, and reclaiming of people barbarous to civility and humanity, we have, by our letters patents, bearing date at Westminster the three and twentieth day of May, in the seventh year of our reign of England, France, and Ireland . . . given and granted unto them, that they, and all such and so many of our loving subjects, as should from time to time for ever after be joined with them as planters or adventurers in the said plantation, and their successors, for ever, should be one body politic, incorporated by the name of The Treasurer and Company of Adventurers and Planters of the city of London for the first Colony in Virginia.

II. And whereas also, for the great good and benefit of the said company, and for the better furtherance, strengthening, and establishing of the said plantation, we did further give . . . unto the said treasurer and company . . . all those lands, countries, or territories situate . . . in that part of America called Virginia, from the point of land called Cape or Point Comfort, all along the sea coasts, to the northward, two hundred miles, and from the said point of Cape Comfort all along the sea coast to the southward, two hundred miles, and all that space and circuit of land lying from the sea coast of the precinct aforesaid, up or into the land, throughout from sea to sea, west and north-west, and also all the islands lying within one hundred miles, along the coast of both the seas of the precinct aforesaid. . . .

III. Now, forasmuch . . . that in those seas adjoining to the said coast of Virginia, and without the compass of those two hundred miles, . . .

there are, or may be, divers islands, lying desolate and uninhabited, . . . all and every of which it may import the said colony, both in safety and policy of trade, to populate and plant. . . .

IV. We therefore . . . do . . . give, grant, and confirm, to the said treasurer and company of adventurers and planters of the city of London for the first colony in Virginia, and to their heirs and successors, for ever, all and singular those islands whatsoever, situate and being in any part of the ocean seas bordering upon the coast of our said first colony in Virginia, and being within three hundred leagues of any the parts heretofore granted . . .: Provided always, that the said islands . . . be not actually possessed or inhabited by any other Christian prince or estate, nor be within the bounds, limits, or territories of the northern colony heretofore by us granted to be planted by divers of our loving subjects, in the north parts of Virginia. To have and to hold . . . to be holden of us, our heirs, and successors, as of our manor of East Greenwich, in free and common socage, and not *in capite*; yielding and paying therefore to us, our heirs, and successors, the fifth part of the ore of all gold and silver which shall be there gotten, had, or obtained, for all manner of services whatsoever.

V. [Names new members of the company.]

VI. [Appoints several men to the council for the colony.]

VII. And we do hereby ordain . . . that the said treasurer and company of adventurers and planters aforesaid, shall and may, once every week or oftener, at their pleasure, hold and keep a court and assembly for the better order and government of the said plantation, and such things as shall concern the same; and that any five persons of our council for the said first colony in Virginia . . . of which company the treasurer, or his deputy, to be always one, and the number of fifteen others at the least of the generality of the said company . . . and shall be a sufficient court of the said company for the handling, and ordering, and dispatching of all such casual and particular occurrences . . . as shall from time to time happen, touching and concerning the said plantation.

VIII. And that nevertheless, for the handling, ordering, and disposing of matters and affairs of greater weight and importance . . . as namely the manner of government from time to time to be used, the ordering and disposing of the lands and possessions, and the settling and establishing of a trade there, or such like, there shall be held and kept, every year, upon the last Wednesday save one of Hilary term,

Easter, Trinity, and Michaelmas terms, for ever, one great, general, and solemn assembly, which four assemblies shall be styled and called, The Four Great and General Courts of the Council and Company of Adventurers for Virginia; in all and every of which said great and general courts so assembled . . . they, the said treasurer and company, or the greater number of them so assembled, shall and may have full power and authority . . . to elect and choose discreet persons to be of our said council, for the said first colony in Virginia, and to nominate and appoint such officers as they shall think fit and requisite for the government . . . of the affairs of the said company, and shall likewise have full power and authority to ordain and make such laws and ordinances for the good and welfare of the said plantation, as to them, from time to time, shall be thought requisite and meet: so always, as the same be not contrary to the laws and statutes of this our realm of England; and shall, in like manner, have power and authority to expulse, disfranchise, and put out of and from their said company . . . all and every such person and persons as having either promised, or subscribed their names, to become adventurers to the said plantation . . . have refused and neglected, or shall refuse and neglect, to bring in his or their adventure, by word or writing promised, within six months after the same shall be so payable and due.

IX. And whereas the failing and not payment of such moneys as have been promised in adventure for the advancement of the said plantation hath been often by experience found to be dangerous and prejudicial to the same . . . therefore our will and pleasure is that in any suit or suits commenced . . . by the said treasurer and company, or otherwise, against any such persons, that our judges for the time being, both in our court of chancery, and at the common pleas, do favour and further the said suits, so far forth as law and equity will, in any wise, further and permit.

X. And we do . . . further give and grant to the said treasurer and company, or their successors, for ever, that they . . . shall and may . . . elect, choose, and admit into their company and society any person or persons . . . being in amity with us, as our natural liege subjects, born in any our realms and dominions; and that all such persons so elected, chosen, and admitted to be of the said company, as aforesaid, shall thereupon be taken, reputed, and held, and shall be, free members of the said company, and shall have, hold, and enjoy all and singular freedoms . . . whatsoever to the said company in any sort belonging or appertaining. . . .

XI. And we do further . . . give and grant unto the said treasurer and company . . . that it shall be lawful and free for them and their assigns . . . to take, lead, carry, and transport, in and into the said voyage, and for and towards the said plantation of our said first colony in Virginia, all such and so many of our loving subjects, or any other strangers, that will become our loving subjects and live under our allegiance, as shall willingly accompany them in the said voyages and plantation; with shipping, armour, weapons . . . and all other things necessary for the said plantation, and for their use and defence, and for trade with the people there, and in passing and returning to and from, without paying or yielding any subsidy . . . or any other duty, to us, our heirs, or successors, for the same, for the space of seven years from the date of these presents.

XII. And we do further . . . give and grant . . . that the said treasurer of that company, or his deputy . . . have full power and authority to minister and give the oath and oaths of supremacy and allegiance . . . to all and every person and persons, which shall at any time or times hereafter go or pass to the said colony in Virginia.

XIII. And further, that it shall be lawful likewise for the said treasurer, or his deputy, . . . to minister such a formal oath as by their discretion shall be reasonably devised, as well unto any person or persons employed in, for, or touching the said plantation, for their honest, faithful, and just discharge of their service, in all such matters as shall be committed unto them for the good and benefit of the said company. . . .

XIV. And furthermore, whereas we have been certified that divers lewd and ill-disposed persons, both sailors, soldiers, artificers, husbandmen, labourers, and others, having received wages, apparel, and other entertainment from the said company, or having contracted and agreed with the said company to go, or to serve, or to be employed in the said plantation of the said first colony in Virginia, have afterwards either withdrawn, hid or concealed themselves, or have refused to go thither, after they have been so entertained and agreed withal; and that divers and sundry persons also, which have been sent and employed in the said plantation of the said first colony in Virginia, at and upon the charge of the said company, and having there misbehaved themselves by mutinies, sedition, or other notorious misdemeanours, or having been employed or sent abroad by the governor of Virginia, or his deputy, with some ship or pinnace, for our provision of the said colony, or for some discovery, or other business and affairs concerning the same, have from thence most treacherously either come back again and returned unto our realm of England by stealth, . . . and others, for the colouring of their lewdness and misdemeanours committed in Virginia, have endeavoured by most vile and slanderous reports . . . to bring the said voyage and plantation into disgrace and contempt; by means whereof not only the adventurers and planters already engaged in the said plantation, have been exceedingly abused and hindered, and a great number of other our loving and well disposed subjects, otherwise well affected and inclined to join and adventure in so noble, Christian, and worthy an action, have been discouraged from the same, but also the utter overthrow and ruin of the said enterprise hath been greatly endangered, which cannot miscarry without some dishonour to us and our kingdom.

XV. Now, forasmuch as it appeareth unto us that these insolences, misdemeanours, and abuses, not to be tolerated in any civil government, have, for the most part, grown and proceeded in regard our said council have not any direct power and authority, by any express words in our former letters patents, to correct and chastise such offenders; we therefore, for the more speedy reformation of so great and enormous abuses and misdemeanours . . . do . . . give and grant to the said treasurer and company . . . by warrant under their hands, to send for, or to cause to be apprehended, all and every such person and persons, who shall be noted . . . to offend or misbehave themselves in any the offences before mentioned and expressed; . . . that in all such cases they, our said council . . . shall and may have full power and authority, either here to bind them over with good sureties, for their good behaviour, and further therein to proceed, to all intents and purposes, as it is used, in other like cases, within our realm of England; or else, at their discretion, to remand and send them back, the said offenders, or any of them, unto the said colony in Virginia, there to be proceeded against and punished, as the governor, deputy or council there, for the time being, shall think meet; or otherwise according to such laws and ordinances as are and shall be in use there, for the well ordering and good government of the said colony.

XVI. And for the more effectual advancing of the said plantation we do further, . . . give and grant unto the said treasurer and company full power and authority, . . . to set forth, erect, and publish one or more lottery or lotteries, to have continuance, . . . during our will and pleasure only, and not otherwise. . . .

XVII. And our further will and pleasure is that the said lottery and lotteries shall and may be opened and held within our city of London, or in any other city or town, or elsewhere, within this our realm of England. . . .

XVIII. And that it shall and may be lawful, to and for the said treasurer and company, to elect and choose receivers, auditors, surveyors, commissioners, or any other officers whatsoever, at their will and pleasure, for the better marshalling, disposing, guiding, and governing of the said lottery and lotteries. . . .

XIX. And we further grant . . . that it shall and may be lawful, to and for the said treasurer and company, under the seal of the said council for the plantation, to publish, or to cause and procure to be published, by proclamation or otherwise . . . the said lottery or lotteries in all cities, towns, boroughs, and other places within our said realm of England. . . .

XX. And further our will and pleasure is, that in all questions and doubts that shall arise upon any difficulty of construction or interpretation of anything contained in these, or any other our former letters patents, the same shall be taken and interpreted in most ample and beneficial manner for the said treasurer and company, and their successors, for ever, and every member thereof.

XXI. And lastly, we do by these presents ratify and confirm unto the said treasurer and company . . . all manner of privileges . . . and commodities whatsoever granted unto them in any our former letters patents, and not in these presents revoked, altered, changed, or abridged . . . or any statute . . . or restraint, to the contrary thereof heretofore made . . . to the contrary in any wise notwithstanding.

> Original version of the charter is lost. Copy reprinted in *The Statutes at Large . . . of Virginia*, ed. W. W. Hening (1809-23), i.98-110

3   First Legislative Assembly in North America, 1619

Sir George Yeardley, governor of Virginia, called a representative assembly of the colonists to meet at Jamestown on 30 July 1619. This was the first legislative assembly called together in North America and marks the beginning of American popular government. The governor of the colony retained the right to veto actions of the assembly. A report of the meeting, dissolved on 4 August, was sent to the Virginia Company of London by John Pory, secretary of the colony. Excerpts from his report are reprinted below.

A report of the manner of proceeding in the General Assembly convened at James City in Virginia, July 30, 1619, consisting of the Governor, the Council of Estate, and two Burgesses, elected out of each incorporation and plantation, and being dissolved the 4th of August next ensuing.

First, Sir George Yeardley, Knight, Governor and Captain-General of Virginia, having sent his summons all over the country, as well to invite those of the Council of Estate that were absent as also for the election of burgesses, there were chosen and appeared:

[List of representatives for 11 townships]

The most convenient place we could find to sit in was the choir of the church where Sir George Yeardley, the governor, being set down in his accustomed place, those of the Council of Estate sat next him on both hands except only the secretary, then appointed speaker, who sat right before him, John Twine, clerk of the General Assembly, being placed next the speaker, and Thomas Pierse, the sergeant, standing at the bar, to be ready for any service the Assembly should command him. . . . Every man . . . took the oath of supremacy, and then entered the Assembly. At Captain Warde, the speaker took exception, as at one that without any commission or authority had seated himself, either upon the company's, and then his plantation could not be lawful, or on Captain Martin's land, and so he was but a limb or member of him, and so there could be but two burgesses for all. So Captain Warde was commanded to absent himself till such time as the Assembly had agreed what was fit for him to do. After much debate, they resolved on this order following:

An order concluded by the General Assembly concerning Captain Warde, July 30th, 1619, at the opening of the said Assembly.

At the reading of the names of the burgesses, exception was taken against Captain Warde as having planted here in Virginia without any authority or commission from the treasurer, council, and company in England. But considering he had been at so great charge and pains to augment this colony, and had adventured his own person in the action, and since that time had brought home a good quantity of fish, to relieve the colony by way of trade, and above all, because the commission for authorizing the General Assembly admitteth of two burgesses out of every plantation without restraint or exception: upon all these considerations, the Assembly was contented to admit of him and his lieutenant (as members of their body and burgesses) into their society. Provided, that the said Captain Warde with all expedition, that is to say between this and the next General Assembly (all lawful impediments excepted), should procure from the treasurer, council, and company in England a commission lawfully to establish and plant himself and his company as the chiefs of other plantations have done. And in case he do neglect this he is to stand to the censure of the next General Assembly. To this Captain Warde, in the presence of us all, having given his consent and undertaken to perform the same, was, together with his lieutenant, by the voices of the whole Assembly, first admitted to take the oath of supremacy, and then to make up their number and to sit amongst them.

[The governor questions the right of Captain Martin's burgesses to sit in the Assembly because of a clause in Martin's patent.]

Upon the motion of the governor, discussed the same time in the Assembly, ensued this order following:

An order of the General Assembly touching a clause in Captain Martin's patent at James City, July 30, 1619.

After all the burgesses had taken the oath of supremacy and were admitted into the house and all set down in their places, a copy of Captain Martin's patent was produced by the governor out of a clause whereof it appeared that when the General Assembly had made some kind of laws requisite for the whole colony, he and his burgesses and people might deride the whole company and choose whether they would obey the same or no. It was therefore ordered in court that the aforesaid two burgesses should withdraw themselves out of the Assembly till such time as Captain Martin had made his personal appearance before them. At what time, if upon their motion, if he would be content to quit and give over that part of his patent, and contrary thereunto would submit himself to the general form of government as all others did, that then his burgesses should be readmitted, otherwise they were utterly to be excluded as being spies rather than loyal burgesses, because they had offered themselves to be assistant at the making of laws which both themselves and those whom they represented might choose whether they would obey or not.

Then came in a complaint against Captain Martin, that having sent his shallop to trade for corn into the bay, under the command of Ensign Harrison, the said ensign should affirm to one Thomas Davis, of Paspaheighs, Gent. (as the said Thomas Davis deposed upon oath) that they had made a hard voyage, had they not met with a canoe coming out of a creek where their shallop could not go. For the Indians refusing to sell their corn, those of the shallop entered the canoe with their arms and took it by force, measuring out the corn with a basket they had into the shallop and, as the said Ensign Harrison saith, giving them satisfaction in copper beads and other trucking stuff.

Hitherto Mr. Davis upon his oath.

Furthermore it was signified from Opechancanough to the governor that those people had complained to him to procure them justice. For which considerations and because such outrages as this might breed danger and loss of life to others of the colony which should have leave to trade in the bay hereafter, and for prevention of the like violences against the Indians in time to come, this order following was agreed on by the General Assembly:

A second order made against Captain Martin, at James City, July 30, 1619.

It was also ordered by the Assembly the same day that in case Captain Martin and the ging [crew] of his shallop could not thoroughly answer an accusation of an outrage committed against a certain canoe of Indians in the bay, that then it was thought reason (his patent notwithstanding, the authority whereof he had in that case abused), he should from henceforth take leave of the Governor as other men, and should put in security that his people shall commit no such outrage any more.

Upon this a letter or warrant was drawn in the name of the whole Assembly to summon Captain Martin to appear before them in the form following:

By the Governor and General Assembly of Virginia. . . .
Having thus prepared them he [the speaker] read over unto them the great charter, or commission of privileges, orders, and laws sent by Sir George Yeardley out of England.
Which for the more ease of the committees, having divided into four books, he read the former two the same forenoon, for expedition's sake

a second time over, and so they were referred to the perusal of two committees, which did reciprocally consider of either, and accordingly brought in their opinions. But some man may here object to what end we should presume to refer that to the examination of committees which the council and company in England had already resolved to be perfect, and did expect nothing but our assent thereunto. To this we answer that we did it not to the end to correct or control anything therein contained, but only in case we should find aught not perfectly squaring with the state of this colony or any law which did press or bind too hard, that we might by way of humble petition seek to have it redressed, especially because this great charter is to bind us and our heirs for ever. . . .

After dinner the governor and those that were not of the committees sat a second time, while the said committees were employed in the perusal of those two books. And whereas the speaker had propounded four several objects for the Assembly to consider on: namely, first, the great charter of orders, laws, and privileges; secondly, which of the instructions given by the council in England to my Lord de la Warr, Captain Argall, or Sir George Yeardley, might conveniently put on the habit of laws; thirdly, what laws might issue out of the private conceit of any of the burgesses, or any other of the colony; and lastly, what petitions were fit to be sent home for England. It pleased the governor for expedition['s] sake to have the second object of the four to be examined and prepared by himself and the non-committee. Wherein, after having spent some three hours['] conference, the two committees brought in their opinions concerning the two former books (the second of which beginneth at these words of the charter: And forasmuch as our intent is to establish one equal and uniform kind of government over all Virginia etc.) which the whole Assembly because it was late, deferred to treat of till the next morning.

Saturday July 31

The next day, therefore, out of the opinions of the said committees, it was agreed, those petitions ensuing should be framed, to be presented to the treasurer, council, and company in England. Upon the committees' perusal of the first book, the General Assembly do become most humble suitors to their lordships and to the rest of that honourable council and renowned company, that albeit they have been pleased to allot unto the governor to themselves, together with the Council of Estate here, and to the officers of incorporations, certain large portions of land to be laid out within the limits of the same, yet that they would vouchsafe also, that such grounds as heretofore hath been granted by patent to the ancient planters by former governors that had from the company received commission so to do, might not now after so much labour and cost, and so many years habitation be taken from them. And to the end that no man might do or suffer any wrong in this kind, that they would favour us so much (if they mean to grant this our petition) as to send us notice, what commission or authority for granting of lands they have given to each particular governor in times past.

The second petition of the General Assembly framed by the committees out of the second book is that the treasurer and company in England would be pleased with as much convenient speed as may be to send men hither to occupy their lands belonging to the four incorporations, as well for their own behoof and profit as for the maintenance of the Council of Estate, who are now to their extreme hindrance often drawn far from their private business and likewise that they will have a care to send tenants to the ministers of the four incorporations to manure their glebe, to the intent that the allowance they have allotted them of £200 a year may the more easily be raised.

The third petition humbly presented by this General Assembly to the treasurer, council, and company is that it may plainly be expressed in the great commission (as indeed it is not) that the ancient planters of both sorts, viz., such as before Sir Thomas Dale's departure were come hither upon their own charges, and such also as were brought hither upon the company's cost, may have their second, third, and more divisions successively in as large and free manner as any other planters. Also that they will be pleased to allow to the male children, of them and of all others begotten in Virginia, being the only hope of a posterity, a single share apiece, and shares for their wives as for themselves, because that in a new plantation it is not known whether man or woman be the most necessary.

Their fourth petition is to beseech the treasurer, council, and company that they would be pleased to appoint a sub-treasurer here to collect their rents, to the end that the inhabitants of this colony be not tied to an impossibility of paying the same yearly to the treasurer in England, and that they would enjoin the said sub-treasurer not precisely according to the letter of the charter to exact money of us (whereof we have none at all, as we have no mint), but the true value of the rent in commodity.

The fifth petition is to beseech the treasurer, council, and company that, towards the erecting of the university and college, they will send, when they shall think most convenient, workmen of all sorts, fit for that purpose.

The sixth and last is, they will be pleased to change the savage name of Kiccowtan, and to give that incorporation a new name. [It was later changed to Elizabeth City.] ...

These petitions thus concluded on, those two committees brought in a report what they had observed in the two latter books, which was nothing else but that the perfection of them was such as they could find nothing therein subject to exception, only the governor's particular opinion to myself in private hath been as touching a clause in the third book, that in these doubtful times between us and the Indians, it would behoove us not to make so large distances between plantation and plantation as ten miles, but for our more strength and security to draw nearer together. At the same time, there remaining no farther scruple in the minds of the Assembly touching the said great charter of laws, orders, and privileges, the speaker put the same to the question, and so it had both the general assent and the applause of the whole Assembly, who, as they professed themselves in the first place most submissively thankful to Almighty God, therefore so they commanded the speaker to return (as now he doth) their due and humble thanks to the treasurer, council, and company for so many privileges and favours as well in their own names as in the names of the whole colony whom they represented.

[Price of tobacco set at 3s. for the best and 'the second sort at 8d. the pound'.]

Monday, August 2
[Consideration of Captain John Martin's patent.]

The premises about Captain Martin thus resolved, the committee appointed to consider what instructions are fit to be converted into laws, brought in their opinions, and first of some of the general instructions.

> Here begin the laws drawn out of the instructions given by his Majesty's Council of Virginia in England to my Lord de la War, Captain Argall, and Sir George Yeardley, Knight.

By this present General Assembly be it enacted that no injury or oppression be wrought by the English against the Indians whereby the present peace might be disturbed and ancient quarrels might be revived. And further be it ordained that the Chickahominy are not to be excepted out of this law, until either that such order come out of England, or that they do provoke us by some new injury.

Against idleness, gaming, drunkenness, and excess in apparel the Assembly hath enacted as followeth:

First, in detestation of idlers be it enacted, that if any man be found to live as an idler or runagate, though a freedman, it shall be lawful for that incorporation or plantation to which he belongeth to appoint him a master to serve for wages till he show apparent signs of amendment.

Against gaming at dice and cards be it ordained by this present Assembly that the winner or winners shall lose all his or their winnings, and both winners and losers shall forfeit ten shillings a man, one ten shillings whereof to go to the discoverer, and the rest to charitable and pious uses in the incorporation where the faults are committed.

Against drunkenness be it also decreed that if any private person be found culpable thereof, for the first time he is to be reproved privately by the minister, the second time publicly, the third time to lie in bolts 12 hours in the house of the provost-marshal and to pay his fees, and if he still continue in that vice, to undergo such severe punishment as the governor and Council of Estate shall think fit to be inflicted on him. . . .

Against excess of apparel that every man be cessed in the church for all public contributions, if he be unmarried according to his own apparel; if he be married, according to his own and his wife's, or either of their apparel.

As touching the instruction of drawing some of the better disposed of the Indians to converse with out people and to live and labour amongst them, the Assembly who know well their dispositions think it fit to enjoin, at least to counsel those of the colony, neither utterly to reject them nor yet to draw them to come in. But in case they will of themselves come voluntarily to places well peopled, there to do service in killing of deer, fishing, beating corn, and other works, that then five or six may be admitted into every such place, and no more, and that with the consent of the governor. Provided that good guard in the night be kept upon them, for generally (though some amongst many may prove good) they are a most treacherous people and quickly gone when they have done a villainy. And it were fit a house were built for them to lodge in apart by themselves, and lone inhabitants by no means to entertain them.

Be it enacted by this present Assembly that for laying a surer foundation of the conversion of the Indians to Christian religion, each town, city, borough, and particular plantation do obtain unto themselves by just means a certain number of the natives' children to be educated by them in true religion and civil course of life, of which children the most towardly boys in wit and graces of nature to be brought up by them in the first elements of literature, so as to be fitted for the college intended for them that from thence they may be sent to that work of conversion.

As touching the business of planting corn this present Assembly doth ordain that year by year all and every householder and householders have in store for every servant he or they shall keep, and also for his or their own persons, whether they have any servants or no, one spare barrel of corn to be delivered out yearly, either upon sale or exchange as need shall require. For the neglect of which duty he shall be subject to the censure of the governor and Council of Estate. Provided always that the first year of every new man this law shall not be of force.

About the plantation of mulberry trees, be it enacted that every man as he is seated upon his division, do for seven years together, every year plant and maintain in growth six mulberry trees at the least, and as many more as he shall think convenient, and as his virtue and industry shall move him to plant, and that all such persons as shall neglect the yearly planting and maintaining of that small proportion shall be subject to the censure of the governor and the Council of Estate.

[Enactments for the cultivation of silk, flax, hemp, anise, and vineyards.]

Be it also enacted that all necessary tradesmen, or so many as need shall require, such as are come over since the departure of Sir Thomas Dale, or that shall hereafter come, shall work at their trades for any other man, each one being paid according to the quality of his trade and work, to be estimated, if he shall not be contented, by the governor and officers of the place where he worketh.

Be it further ordained by this General Assembly, and we do by these presents enact, that all contracts made in England between the owners of the land and their tenants and servants which they shall send hither, may be caused to be duly performed, and that the offenders be punished as the governor and Council of Estate shall think just and convenient.

Be it established also by this present Assembly that no crafty or advantageous means be suffered to be put in practice for the enticing away the tenants and servants of any particular plantation from the place where they are seated. And that it shall be the duty of the governor and Council of Estate most severely to punish both the seducers and the seduced, and to return these latter into their former places.

Be it further enacted that the orders for the magazine lately made be exactly kept, and that the magazine be preserved from wrong and sinister practices, and that according to the orders of court in England, all tobacco and sassafras be brought by the planters to the cape merchant till such time as all the goods now or heretofore sent for the magazine be taken off their hands at the prices agreed on. That by this means the same going for England into one hand, the price thereof may be upheld the better. And to that end that all the whole colony may take notice of the last order of court made in England, and all those whom it concerneth may know how to observe it, we hold it fit to publish it here for a law among the rest of our laws. The which order is as followeth: . . .

[Restatement of an order sent out by the Council of the Colony in London for the reformation of abuses concerning stores in the magazine or common warehouse.]

Tuesday, August 3, 1619

This morning a third sort of laws (such as might proceed out of every man's private conceit) were read and referred by halves to the same committees which were from the beginning.

This done, Captain William Powell presented to the Assembly a petition to have justice against a lewd and treacherous servant of his, who, by false accusation given up in writing to the governor, sought not only to get him deposed from his government of James City and utterly (according to the proclamation) to be degraded from the place and title of a captain, but to take his life from him also. And so out of the said petition sprang this order following: . . .

It was thought fit by the General Assembly (the governor himself giving sentence) that he should stand four days with his ears nailed to the pillory, viz.: Wednesday, August 4, and so likewise Thursday, Friday, and Saturday next following, and every of those four days should be publicly whipped. Now, as touching the neglect of his work, what satisfaction ought to be made to his master for that is referred to the governor and Council of Estate. . . .

This afternoon the committees brought in a report what they had done as concerning the third sort of laws, the discussing whereof spent the residue of that day. Except only the consideration of a petition of Mr. John Rolfe against Captain John Martin for writing a letter to him wherein (as Mr. Rolfe alleges) he taxeth him both unseemly and amiss of certain things wherein he was never faulty, and besides, casteth some aspersion upon the present government, which is the most temperate and just that ever was in this country, too mild indeed, for many of this colony whom unwonted liberty has made insolent and not to know themselves. This petition of Mr. Rolfe's was thought fit to be referred to the Council of State.

Wednesday, August 4th

This day (by reason of extreme heat, both past and likely to ensue, and by that means of the alteration of the healths of divers of the General Assembly) the governor, who himself also was not well, resolved should be the last of this first session; so in the morning the speaker (as he was required by the Assembly) read over all the laws and orders that had formerly passed the house, to give the same yet one review more, and to see whether there were anything to be amended or that might be excepted against. This being done, the third sort of laws which I am now coming to set down, were read over and thoroughly discussed, which, together with the former, did now pass the last and final consent of the General Assembly.

A third sort of laws, such as may issue out of every man's private conceits.

It shall be free for every man to trade with the Indians, servants only excepted, upon pain of whipping, unless the master redeem it off with the payment of an angel, one fourth part whereof to go to the provost-marshal, one fourth part to the discoverer, and the other moiety to the public uses of the incorporation.

That no man do sell or give any Indians any piece, shot, or powder, or any other arms, offensive or defensive, upon pain of being held a traitor to the colony, and of being hanged as soon as the fact is proved, without all redemption.

That no man do sell or give any of the greater hoes to the Indians, or any English dog of quality, as a mastiff, greyhound, bloodhound, land or water spaniel, or any other dog or bitch whatsoever, of the English race, upon pain of forfeiting £5 sterling to the public uses of the incorporation where he dwelleth.

That no man may go above twenty miles from his dwelling-place, nor upon any voyage whatsoever shall be absent from thence for the space of seven days together without first having made the governor or commander of the same place acquainted therewith, upon pain of paying twenty shillings to the public uses of the same incorporation where the party delinquent dwelleth.

That no man shall purposely go to any Indian towns, habitations, or places of resort without leave from the governor or commander of that place where he liveth, upon pain of paying 40s. to public uses as aforesaid.

[Every man to register himself and his servants with the secretary of state before 1 January.]

[All ministers to report vital statistics of their parishes, in March.]

No man, without leave of the governor, shall kill any neat cattle whatsoever, young or old, especially kine, heifers or cow-calves, and shall be careful to preserve their steers and oxen, and to bring them to the plough and such profitable uses, and without having obtained leave as aforesaid, shall not kill them, upon penalty of forfeiting the value of the beast so killed.

[Penalties for stealing, or borrowing without leave.]
[Ministers to hold services according to the 'laws and orders of the Church of England', and to 'prevent all ungodly disorders'.]

If any person after two warnings do not amend his or her life in point of evident suspicion of incontinency or of the commission of any other enormous sins, that then he or she be presented by the churchwardens and suspended for a time from the church by the minister. In which interim, if the same person do not amend and humbly submit him or herself to the church, he is then fully to be excommunicate and soon after a writ or warrant to be sent from the governor for the apprehending of his person and seizing all his goods. . . .

For reformation of swearing, every freeman and master of a family, after thrice admonition, shall give 5s. or the value upon present demand to the use of the church where he dwelleth; and every servant after the like admonition, except his master discharge the fine, shall be subject to whipping. Provided, that the payment of the fine notwithstanding, the said servant shall acknowledge his fault publicly in the church.

No man whatsoever, coming by water from above . . . and being bound for Kiccowtan, or any other part on this side, the same shall presume to pass by, either by day or by night, without touching first here at James City to know whether the governor will command him any service. And the like shall they perform that come from Kiccowtanward . . . upon pain of forfeiting ten pound sterling a time to the governor . . . .

No man shall trade into the bay, either in shallop, pinnace, or ship, without the governor's licence, and without putting in security that neither himself nor his company shall force or wrong the Indians, upon pain that, doing otherwise, they shall be censured at their return by the governor and Council of Estate.

All persons whatsoever upon the Sabbath day shall frequent divine service and sermons both forenoon and afternoon, and all such as bear arms shall bring their pieces, swords, powder and shot. And everyone that shall transgress this law shall forfeit three shillings a time to the use of the church, all lawful and necessary impediments excepted. But if a servant in this case shall wilfully neglect his master's command he shall suffer bodily punishment.

No maid or woman servant, either now resident in the colony or hereafter to come, shall contract herself in marriage without either the consent of her parents, or her master or mistress, or of the magistrate and minister of the place both together. And whatsoever minister shall marry or contract any such persons without some of the foresaid consents shall be subject to the severe censure of the governor and Council of Estate.

Be it enacted by this present Assembly that whatsoever servant hath heretofore or shall hereafter contract himself in England, either by way of indenture or otherwise, to serve any master here in Virginia, and shall afterward, against his said former contract, depart from his master without leave, or being once embarked, shall abandon the ship he is appointed to come in, and so being left behind, shall put himself into the service of any other man that will bring him hither, that then at the same servant's arrival here, he shall first serve out his time with that master that brought him hither and afterward also shall serve out his time with his former master according to his covenant.

Here end the laws.

[Consideration of a charge of misdemeanours brought against Henry Spelman; other matters considered.]

The last act of the General Assembly was a contribution to gratify their officers as follows:

It is fully agreed at this General Assembly that in regard of the great pains and labour of the speaker [John Pory, author of this report] of this Assembly . . . and likewise in respect of the diligence of the clerk and sergeant, officers thereto belonging: that every man and man-servant of above 16 years of age shall pay into the hands and custody of the burgesses of every incorporation and plantation, one pound of the best tobacco, to be distributed to the speaker and likewise to the clerk and sergeant of the Assembly, according to their degrees and ranks, the whole bulk whereof to be delivered into the speaker's hands, to be divided accordingly. And in regard to the provost-marshal of James City hath also given some attendance upon the said General Assembly, he is also to have a share out of the same. And this is to begin to be gathered the 24th of February next.

In conclusion, the whole Assembly commanded the speaker (as now he doth) to present their humble excuse to the treasurer, council, and company in England for being constrained by the intemperature of the weather and the falling sick of divers of the burgesses, to break up so abruptly – before they had so much as put their laws to the engrossing. This they wholly committed to the fidelity of their speaker, who therein (his conscience tells him) hath done the part of an honest man; otherwise he would be easily found out by the burgesses themselves, who with all expedition are to have so many books of the same laws as there are both incorporations and plantations in the colony. . . .

Their last humble suit is that the said council and company would be pleased, so soon as they shall find it convenient, to make good their promise set down at the conclusion of their commission for establishing the Council of Estate and the General Assembly, namely, that they will give us power to allow or disallow of their orders of court, as his Majesty has given them power to allow or to reject our laws.

In sum, Sir George Yeardley, the governor prorogued the said General Assembly till the first of March, which is to fall out this present year of 1619, and in the mean season dissolved the same.

Narratives of Early Virginia, 1606–1625 ('Original Narratives of Early American History' series), ed. L. G. Tyler (1907), pp. 249–78

4   The Mayflower Compact, 1620

When the group of Separatists now known as the 'Pilgrims' arrived off Plymouth, Massachusetts, in December 1620, and decided to settle there, they realized that they were beyond the jurisdiction of the Virginia Company. They therefore were under no charter and had no laws to govern them. Some of the more ungodly from London who had been allowed to join the company boasted that they would 'use their own liberty' once they were on land. Therefore, before anyone was permitted to go ashore, a meeting was held and a brief statement of political policy was drawn up and signed by forty-one men.

In the name of God, Amen. We whose names are underwritten, the loyal subjects of our dread Sovereign Lord, King James, by the grace of God of Great Britain, France, and Ireland King, Defender of the Faith, etc.: Having undertaken, for the glory of God and advancement of the Christian faith and honour of our king and country, a voyage to plant the first colony in the northern parts of Virginia, do, by these presents, solemnly and mutually in the presence of God and one of another, covenant and combine ourselves together into a civil body politic for our better ordering and preservation and furtherance of the ends aforesaid. And by virtue hereof to enact, constitute, and frame such just and equal laws, ordinances, acts, constitutions, and offices, from time to time, as shall be thought most meet and convenient for the general good of the colony; unto which we promise all due submission and obedience. In witness whereof we have hereunder subscribed our names at Cape Cod the 11th of November, in the year of the reign of our Sovereign Lord King James, of England, France, and Ireland the eighteenth, and of Scotland the fifty-fourth. Anno Domini 1620.

Mr. John Carver
Mr. William Bradford
Mr. Edward Winslow
Mr. William Brewster
Isaac Allerton
Miles Standish
John Alden
et al.

> William Bradford, *History of the Plymouth Plantation* (MS. ca. 1630-48). First printed in *Collections of Massachusetts Historical Soc.* (ed. C. Deane, 1856). Frequently reprinted

5   Maryland Charter, 1632

On 20 June 1632 Charles I issued to Caecilius Calvert, Baron Baltimore, a charter making him lord proprietor of the Province of Maryland, lying between Virginia and Pennsylvania. As proprietor Calvert was owner of the land

and could lease or sell it as he saw fit. The essential sections showing differences of a proprietary charter from others are given below.

... II. [Authorization for colonizing lands occupied by heathen.]

III. [Bounds of land granted Calvert.]

IV. [Islands granted 'within ten marine leagues from the said shore'.]

V. And we do by these presents ... make, create, and constitute him, the now baron of Baltimore, and his heirs, the true and absolute lords and proprietaries of the region aforesaid ... saving always the faith and allegiance and sovereign dominion due to us, our heirs, and successors; ... to the sole and proper behoof and use of him, the now baron of Baltimore, his heirs and assigns, for ever. To hold of us, our heirs, and successors, kings of England, as of our castle of Windsor, in our county of Berks, in free and common socage, by fealty only for all services, and not *in capite*, nor by knight's service, yielding therefore unto us, our heirs, and successors two Indian arrows of those parts, to be delivered at the said castle of Windsor every year, on Tuesday in Easter week; and also the fifth part of all gold and silver ore which shall happen from time to time, to be found within the aforesaid limits. ...

VI. Now, that the aforesaid region ... may be eminently distinguished above all other regions of that territory, and decorated with more ample titles, know ye, that we ... have thought fit that the said region and islands be erected into a province ... and nominate the same Maryland, by which name we will that it shall from henceforth be called.

VII. And forasmuch as we have above made and ordained the aforesaid now baron of Baltimore, the true lord and proprietary of the whole province aforesaid, know ye therefore further, that we ... do grant unto the said now baron ... and to his heirs, for the good and happy government of the said province, free, full, and absolute power by the tenor of these presents, to ordain, make, and enact laws, of what kind soever, according to their sound discretions, whether relating to the public state of the said province or the private utility of individuals, of and with the advice, assent, and approbation of the freemen of the same province ... whom we will shall be called together for the framing of laws, when and as often as need shall require, by the aforesaid now baron of Baltimore, and his heirs, and in the form which shall seem best to him or them, and the same to publish under the seal of the aforesaid now baron of Baltimore, and his heirs, and duly to execute the same upon all persons, for the time being, within the aforesaid province, . . . or under his or their government and power, in sailing towards Maryland, or thence returning, . . . by the imposition of fines, imprisonment, and other punishment whatsoever; even if it be necessary, and the quality of the offence require it, by privation of member, or life, . . . and to constitute and ordain judges, justices, magistrates, and officers, of what kind, for what cause, and with what power soever, within that land, and the sea of those parts, and in such form as to the said now baron of Baltimore, or his heirs, shall seem most fitting; and also to remit, release, pardon, and abolish all crimes and offences whatsoever against such laws, . . . and to do all and singular other things belonging to the completion of justice, . . . although express mention thereof in these presents be not made; . . . which said laws, so to be published as abovesaid, we will, enjoin, charge, and command, to be most absolute and firm in law, and to be kept in those parts by all the subjects and liege men of us, our heirs, and successors, so far as they concern them, and to be inviolably observed under the penalties therein expressed, or to be expressed. So nevertheless, that the laws aforesaid be consonant to reason, and be not repugnant or contrary, but (so far as conveniently may be) agreeable to the laws, statutes, customs and rights of this our kingdom of England.

VIII. [Proprietor authorized to issue decrees with force of law in emergencies.]

IX. [Authorization for lawful subjects to emigrate to Maryland at will, and to build fortified places for their protection 'at the appointment of the aforesaid now baron of Baltimore'.]

X. [All subjects living in Maryland and their descendants to 'be held, treated, reputed, and esteemed as the faithful liege men of us, and our heirs and successors, born within our kingdom of England'.]

XI. [Authority to Maryland to ship 'wares and merchandises, likewise grain of what sort soever, and other things whatsoever necessary for food and clothing . . . not prohibited to be transported out of the said kingdom'.]

XII. [Authority given the proprietor to raise troops when necessary for the defence of Maryland and 'to do all other and singular the things which appertain or have been accustomed to appertain unto the authority and office of captain-general of an army'.]

XIII. [Authority granted the proprietor to declare martial law to suppress sedition or piracy.]

XIV. Moreover, lest in so remote and far distant a region, every access to honours and dignities may seem to be precluded, and utterly barred, to men well born, who are preparing to engage in the present expedition, and desirous of deserving well, both in peace and war, of us, and our kingdom; for this cause, we ... do give free and plenary power to the aforesaid now baron of Baltimore ... to confer favours, rewards, and honours upon such subjects, inhabiting within the province aforesaid, as shall be well deserving, and to adorn them with whatsoever titles and dignities they shall appoint (so that they be not such as are now used in England); also to erect and incorporate towns into boroughs, and boroughs into cities, with suitable privileges and immunities, according to the merits of the inhabitants, and convenience of the places; and to do all and singular other things in the premises, which to him or them shall seem fitting and convenient. ...

XV. We ... give and grant licence by this our charter unto the aforesaid ... freely to import and unlade, by themselves, their servants, factors or assigns, all wares and merchandises whatsoever, which shall be collected out of the fruits and commodities of the said province, whether the product of the land or the sea, into any the ports whatsoever of us, our heirs, and successors, of England or Ireland or otherwise to dispose of the same there; and if need be, within one year, to be computed immediately from the time of unlading thereof, to lade the same merchandises again, in the same, or other ships, and to export the same to any other countries they shall think proper, whether belonging to us, or any foreign power which shall be in amity with us, our heirs or successors: provided always, that they be bound to pay for the same to us, our heirs, and successors, such customs and impositions, subsidies and taxes, as our other subjects of our kingdom of England, for the time being, shall be bound to pay, beyond which we will that the inhabitants of the aforesaid province of the said land, called Maryland, shall not be burdened.

XVI. [Authorization for the establishment of ports in Maryland and the assertion of the rights of all Englishmen to the fisheries within the waters of Maryland.]

XVII. [Authorization of the proprietor to impose taxes and duties 'upon just cause and in due proportion'.]

XVIII. And furthermore ... we ... do give, grant, and confirm ... full and absolute licence, power and authority, that he, the aforesaid now baron of Baltimore, his heirs and assigns, from time to time

ECNA C

hereafter, for ever, may and can, at his or their will and pleasure, assign, alien, grant, demise, or enfeoff so many, such, and proportionate parts and parcels of the premises, to any person or persons willing to purchase the same, as they shall think convenient, to have and to hold . . . in fee-simple or fee-tail or for term of life, lives or years; to hold of the aforesaid now baron of Baltimore, his heirs and assigns, by so many, such, and so great services, customs and rents of this kind, as to the same now baron of Baltimore, his heirs and assigns, shall seem fit and agreeable, and not immediately of us, our heirs and successors. . . .

XIX. We also, by these presents, do give and grant licence to the same baron of Baltimore, and to his heirs, to erect any parcels of land within the province aforesaid, into manors, and in every of those manors, to have and to hold a court-baron, and all things which to a court-baron do belong; and to have and to keep view of frankpledge, for the conservation of the peace and better government of those parts. . . .

XX. And further we will . . . that we, our heirs, and successors, at no time hereafter, will impose, or make or cause to be imposed, any impositions, customs, or other taxations . . . in or upon the residents or inhabitants of the province aforesaid for their goods, lands, or tenements . . . or in or upon any goods or merchandises within the province aforesaid, or within the ports or harbours of the said province, to be laden or unladen; . . . charging all and singular the officers and ministers of us . . . under our heavy displeasure, that they do not at any time presume to attempt any thing to the contrary of the premises, or that may in any wise contravene the same, but that they, at all times, as is fitting, do aid and assist the aforesaid now baron of Baltimore and his heirs, and the aforesaid inhabitants and merchants of the province of Maryland . . . in the fullest use and enjoyment of this our charter.

XXI. [Residents of Maryland 'shall not henceforth be held or reputed a member or part of the land of Virginia, or of any other colony'.]

XXII. [In case of dispute concerning the meaning of any passage in the charter, 'we will, charge, and command . . . that interpretation to be applied always and in all things, and in all courts and judicatories whatsoever to obtain which shall be judged to be the more beneficial, profitable, and favorable to the aforesaid now baron of Baltimore, his heirs and assigns . . .'.]

Laws of Maryland, ed. T. Bacon (1765), reprinted in *Federal and State Constitutions*, ed. F. N. Thorpe (1909), iii.1669-86

6   The Fundamental Orders of Connecticut, 1639

These 'Orders' have been generally recognized by historians as 'the first written constitution' though the more legal-minded insist that they are no more than a body of law. However defined, the *Orders* placed limits upon governmental power and served as a model for subsequent lawmakers. The settlers of the three Connecticut towns had come from Massachusetts.

Forasmuch as it hath pleased the almighty God, by the wise disposition of His divine providence, so to order and dispose of things that we the inhabitants and residents of Windsor, Hartford, and Wethersfield are now cohabiting and dwelling in and upon the river of Connecticut and the lands thereunto adjoining. And well knowing, where a people are gathered together the word of God requires that to maintain the peace and union of such a people there should be an orderly and decent government established according to God . . . do therefore associate and conjoin ourselves to be as one public state or commonwealth. And do, for ourselves and our successors and such as shall be adjoined to us at any time hereafter, enter into combination and confederation together to maintain and preserve the liberty and purity of the gospel of our Lord Jesus which we now profess, as also the discipline of the churches which, according to the truth of the said gospel, is now practised amongst us. As also in our civil affairs to be guided and governed according to such laws . . . as followeth:

1. It is ordered, sentenced, and decreed that there shall be yearly two general assemblies or courts, the one the second Thursday in April, the other the second Thursday in September following. The first shall be called the Court of Election, wherein shall be yearly chosen from time to time so many magistrates and other public officers as shall be found requisite: whereof one to be chosen governor for the year ensuing and until another be chosen, and no other magistrate to be chosen for more than one year, provided always there be six chosen besides the governor . . . which choice shall be made by all that are admitted freemen and have taken the oath of fidelity and do cohabit within this jurisdiction. . . .

2. It is ordered . . . that the election of the aforesaid magistrates shall be on this manner: Every person present and qualified for choice shall bring in (to the persons deputed to receive them) one single paper with the name of him written in it whom he desires to have governor; and he that hath the greatest number of papers shall be governor for that

year. And the rest of the magistrates or public officers to be chosen in this manner: The secretary for the time being shall first read the names of all that are to be put to choice and then shall severally nominate them distinctly, and every one that would have the person nominated to be chosen shall bring in one single paper written upon, and he that would not have him chosen shall bring in a blank; and every one that hath more written papers than blanks shall be a magistrate for that year....

3. It is ordered . . . that the secretary shall not nominate any person . . . which was not propounded in some general court before to be nominated the next election. And to that end it shall be lawful for each of the towns aforesaid by their deputies to nominate any two whom they conceive fit to be put to election, and the court may add so many more as they judge requisite.

4. It is ordered . . . that no person be chosen governor above once in two years, and that the governor be always a member of some approved congregation and formerly of the magistracy within this jurisdiction, and all the magistrates, freemen of this commonwealth....

5. It is ordered . . . that to the aforesaid Court of Election the several towns shall send their deputies, and when the elections are ended they may proceed in any public service as at other courts. Also, the general court in September shall be for making of laws and any other public occasion which concerns the good of the commonwealth.

6.-7. [Procedure for calling the two standing courts and for choosing deputies.]

8. It is ordered . . . that Windsor, Hartford, and Wethersfield shall have power, each town, to send four of their freemen as deputies to every general court. And whatsoever other towns shall be hereafter added to the jurisdiction, they shall send so many deputies as the court shall judge meet, a reasonable proportion to the number of freemen.... Which deputies shall have the power of the whole town to give their votes and allowance to all such laws and orders as may be for the public good and unto which the said towns are to be bound.

9. It is ordered . . . that the deputies thus chosen shall have power and liberty to appoint a time and a place of meeting together before any general court to advise and consult of all such things as may concern the good of the public, as also to examine their own elections.... Also the said deputies shall have power to fine any that shall be disorderly at their meetings, or for not coming in due time or place according to appointment....

10. It is ordered . . . that every general court . . . shall consist of the governor or someone chosen to moderate the court, and four other magistrates at least, with the major part of the deputies of the several towns legally chosen. . . . In which said general courts shall consist the supreme power of the commonwealth, and they only shall have power to make laws or repeal them, to grant levies, to admit of freemen, dispose of lands undisposed of to several towns or persons, and also shall have power to call either court or magistrate or any other person whatsoever into question for any misdemeanor. . . . And also may deal in any other matter that concerns the good of this commonwealth except election of magistrates, which shall be done by the whole body of freemen.

In which court the governor or moderator shall have power to order the court to give liberty of speech and silence unseasonable and disorderly speakings, to put all things to vote, and, in case the vote be equal, to have the casting vote. But none of these courts shall be adjourned or dissolved without the consent of the major part of the court.

11. It is ordered . . . that when any general court upon the occasions of the commonwealth have agreed upon any sum or sums of money to be levied . . . that a committee be chosen to set out and appoint what shall be the proportion of every town to pay of the said levy, provided the committees be made up of an equal number out of each town.

14th January 1638, the 11 orders abovesaid are voted.

> The Federal and State Constitutions, Colonial Charters, [etc.], ed. B. P. Poore (1877), pt. i, pp. 249ff.

7   The Liberties of the Massachusetts Colony in New England, 1641

The 'Body of Liberties' of 1641, compiled by Nathaniel Ward, represents a provisional set of laws approved by the General Court of Massachusetts Bay and designed to be tried for three years before final enactment as the fundamental law of the colony. This compilation apparently was not printed at the time but circulated in manuscript copies. In 1843 Francis C. Gray announced in the *Collections of the Massachusetts Historical Society* that he had discovered a manuscript of Ward's compilation in the Athenaeum. Later printed versions are based on this manuscript. A satisfactory compilation of the laws was finally made and approved by the General Court in 1647 and printed in Cambridge in 1648. A unique copy of this later compilation, *The Laws and Liberties of Massachusetts*, was reprinted by the Harvard University Press for the Henry E. Huntington Library in 1929.

The free fruition of such liberties, immunities, and privileges as humanity, civility, and Christianity call for as due to every man in his place and proportion, without impeachment and infringement, hath ever been and ever will be the tranquillity and stability of churches and commonwealths, and the denial or deprival thereof the disturbance if not the ruin of both.

We hold it therefore our duty and safety . . . to collect and express all such freedoms as for present we foresee may concern us and our posterity after us. . . .

We do therefore this day religiously and unanimously decree and confirm these following rights, liberties, and privileges. . . .

1. No man's life shall be taken away, no man's honour or good name shall be stained, no man's person shall be arrested, restrained, banished, dismembered, not any ways punished, no man shall be deprived of his wife or children, no man's goods or estate shall be taken away from him, nor any way endamaged under colour of law or countenance of authority, unless it be by virtue or equity of some express law of the country warranting the same. . . .

2. Every person within this jurisdiction, whether inhabitant or foreigner, shall enjoy the same justice and law that is general for the plantation. . . .

3. No man shall be urged to take any oath or subscribe any articles, covenants, or remonstrance of a public and civil nature but such as the general court hath considered, allowed, and required.

4. No man shall be punished for not appearing at or before any civil assembly, court, council, magistrate, or officer, nor for the omission of any office or service, if he shall be necessarily hindered by any apparent act or providence of God which he could neither foresee nor avoid, provided that this law shall not prejudice any person of his just cost or damage in any civil action.

5. No man shall be compelled to any public work or service unless the press be grounded upon some act of the general court and have reasonable allowance therefor.

6. No man shall be pressed in person to any office, work, wars, or other public service that is necessarily and sufficiently exempted by any natural or personal impediment, as by want of years, greatness of age, defect of mind, failing of senses, or impotency of limbs.

7. No man shall be compelled to go out of the limits of this plantation upon any offensive wars . . . but only upon such vindictive and defensive wars . . . as shall be enterprised by the counsel and consent of a court general. . . .

8. No man's cattle or goods of what kind soever shall be pressed or taken for any public use or service, unless it be by warrant grounded upon some act of the general court, nor without such reasonable prices and hire as the ordinary rates of the country do afford. . . .

9. No monopolies shall be granted or allowed amongst us but of such new inventions that are profitable to the country, and that for a short time.

10. All our lands and heritages shall be free from all fines and licenses upon alienations and from all heriots, wardships, liveries, primer seisins, yearday and waste, escheats and forfeitures upon the deaths of parents or ancestors. . . .

11. All persons which are of the age of 21 years and of right understanding and memories, whether excommunicate or condemned, shall have full power and liberty to make their wills and testaments. . . .

12. Every man whether inhabitant or foreigner, free or not free, shall have liberty to come to any public court, council, or town meeting, and either by speech or writing to move any lawful, seasonable, and material question, or to present any necessary motion, complaint, petition, bill, or information whereof that meeting hath proper cognizance. . . .

13. No man shall be rated here for any estate or revenue he hath in England or in any foreign parts till it be transported hither.

14. Any conveyance or alienation of land or other estate whatsoever made by any woman that is married, any child under age, idiot or distracted person shall be good if passed and ratified by the consent of a general court.

15. All covinous or fraudulent alienations or conveyances of lands, tenements, or any hereditaments shall be of no validity to defeat any

man from due debts or legacies, or from any just title, claim, or possession of that which is so fraudulently conveyed.

16. Every inhabitant that is a householder shall have free fishing and fowling in any great ponds and bays, coves and rivers, so far as the sea ebbs and flows within the precincts of the town where they dwell, unless the freemen of the same town or the general court have otherwise appropriated them, provided that this shall not be extended to give leave to any man to come upon others' property without their leave.

17. Every man of or within this jurisdiction shall have free liberty, notwithstanding any civil power, to remove both himself and his family, at their pleasure, out of the same. . . .

RIGHTS, RULES AND LIBERTIES CONCERNING JUDICIAL PROCEEDINGS

18. No man's person shall be restrained or imprisoned by any authority whatsoever before the law hath sentenced him thereto, if he can put in sufficient security, bail, or mainprise for his appearance and good behaviour in the meantime, unless it be in crimes capital and contempts in open court, and in such cases where some express act of court doth allow it.

19. [Instructions regarding 'any miscarriage' among the members of a general court.]

20. If any which are to sit as judges in any other court shall demean themselves offensively in the court, the rest of the judges present shall have power to censure him for it. . . .

21. [A warrant must be served six days before the court sits except 'upon extraordinary occasions'.]

22. No man in any suit or action against another shall falsely pretend great debts or damages to vex his adversary. . . .

23.-25. [Limitations of interest, trespass, and 'circumstantial errors' in court proceedings.]

26. Every man that findeth himself unfit to plead his own cause in any court shall have liberty to employ any man against whom the court doth not except to help him, provided he give him no fee or reward for his pains. . . .

27.-28. [Rights of plaintiffs and defendants.]

29. In all actions at law, it shall be the liberty of the plaintiff and defendant by mutual consent to choose whether they will be tried by the bench or by a jury. . . .

30. It shall be in the liberty both of plaintiff and defendant . . . to challenge any of the jurors. . . .

31.-32. [Instructions regarding obscure evidence and impounded goods.]

33. No man's person shall be arrested or imprisoned upon execution or judgement for any debt or fine if the law can find competent means of satisfaction otherwise from his estate. . . .

34. [Injunction against bringing 'frequent and endless suits'.]

35. No man's corn nor hay that is in the field or upon the cart, nor his garden stuff, nor anything subject to present decay shall be taken in any distress, unless he that takes it doth presently bestow it where it may not be embezzled nor suffer spoil or decay, or give security to satisfy the worth thereof if it come to any harm.

36. It shall be in the liberty of every man . . . to make their appeal to the court of assistants, provided they tender their appeal and put in security to prosecute it before the court be ended wherein they were condemned. . . . And every man shall have liberty to complain to the general court of any injustice done him in any court of assistants or other.

37. In all cases where it appears to the court that the plaintiff hath willingly and wittingly done wrong to the defendant in commencing . . . [a] complaint against him, they shall have power to impose upon him a proportionable fine to the use of the defendant. . . .

38. [The right to put testimony in the public record.]

39. In all actions . . . the court shall have power to respite execution for a convenient time. . . .

40. No conveyance . . . whatsoever shall be of validity if it be gotten by illegal violence . . . or any kind of forcible compulsion called duress.

41. Every man that is to answer for any criminal cause . . . shall be heard . . . at the next court that hath proper cognizance thereof. . . .

42. No man shall be twice sentenced by civil justice for one and the same crime, offense, or trespass.

43. No man shall be beaten with above 40 stripes, nor shall any true gentleman, nor any man equal to a gentleman, be punished with whipping unless his crime be very shameful. . . .

44. No man condemned to die shall be put to death within four days next after his condemnation . . . nor shall the body of any man so put to death be unburied 12 hours unless it be in case of anatomy.

45. No man shall be forced by torture to confess any crime against himself nor any other, unless it be in some capital case where he is first fully convicted. . . . After which, if the cause be of that nature that it is very apparent there be other conspirators or confederates with him, then he may be tortured, yet not with such tortures as be barbarous and inhuman.

46. For bodily punishments we allow amongst us none that are inhumane, barbarous, or cruel.

47. No man shall be put to death without the testimony of two or three witnesses or that which is equivalent thereunto.

48. Every inhabitant of the country shall have free liberty to search and view any rules, records, or registers of any court or office except the council, and to have a transcript . . . thereof written, examined, and signed by the hand of the officer of the office paying the appointed fees therefor.

49. No freeman shall be compelled to serve upon juries above two courts in a year, except grand jury men. . . .

50. All jurors shall be chosen continually by the freemen of the town where they dwell.

51. [Method of nominating associates of the assistants.]

52. Children, idiots, distracted persons, and all that are strangers or newcomers to our plantation shall have such allowances and dispensations in any cause . . . as religion and reason require.

53. The age of discretion for passing away of lands . . . or for giving of votes . . . shall be one and twenty years.

54. [Procedure to be followed in case of the refusal by a president of 'any court of assembly' to propose or put an issue to vote, or to pronounce sentence, etc.]

55. In all suits or actions in any court, the plaintiff shall have liberty to

make all the titles and claims to that he sues for he can. And the defendant shall have liberty to plead all the pleas he can in answer. . . .

56. If any man shall behave himself offensively at any town meeting, the rest of the freemen then present shall have power to sentence him for his offense, so be it . . . exceed not twenty shillings.

57. Whensoever any person shall come to any very sudden, untimely, and unnatural death, some assistant, or the constables of the town, shall forthwith summon a jury of twelve freemen to inquire of the cause and manner of their death. . . .

LIBERTIES MORE PECULIARLY CONCERNING THE FREEMEN

58. Civil authority hath power and liberty to see the peace, ordinances, and rules of Christ observed in every church. . . .

59. Civil authority hath power and liberty to deal with any church member in a way of civil justice. . . .

60. No church censure shall degrade or depose any man from any civil dignity, office, or authority he shall have in the commonwealth.

61. No magistrate, juror, officer, or other man shall be bound to inform . . . or reveal any private crime or offense wherein there is no peril or danger to this plantation or any member thereof, when any necessary tie of conscience binds him to secrecy . . . unless it be in case of testimony lawfully required.

62. Any shire or town shall have liberty to choose their deputies whom and where they please for the general court, so be it they be freemen and have taken their oath of fealty and inhabiting in the jurisdiction.

63.-78. [Rights and limitations of freemen in the exercise of their public privileges and duties.]

LIBERTIES OF WOMEN

79. If any man at his death shall not leave his wife a competent portion of his estate, upon just complaint made to the general court she shall be relieved.

80. Every married woman shall be free from bodily correction or stripes by her husband, unless it be in his own defense upon her assault. . . .

LIBERTIES OF CHILDREN

81. When parents die intestate, the elder son shall have a double portion of his whole estate real and personal, unless the general court upon just cause alleged shall judge otherwise.

82. When parents die intestate, having no heirs males of their bodies, their daughters shall inherit as co-partners, unless the general court . . . shall judge otherwise.

83. If any parents shall willfully and unreasonably deny any child timely or convenient marriage, or shall exercise any unnatural severity towards them, such children shall have free liberty to complain to authority for redress.

84. No orphan during their minority, which was not committed to tuition or service by the parents in their lifetime, shall afterwards be absolutely disposed of by any kindred, friend, executor, . . . nor by themselves, without the consent of some court wherein two assistants at least shall be present.

LIBERTIES OF SERVANTS

85. If any servants shall flee from the tyranny and cruelty of their masters to the house of any freeman of the same town, they shall be there protected and sustained until due order be taken for their relief, provided due notice thereof be speedily given to their masters. . . .

86. No servant shall be put off for above a year to any other . . . unless it be by consent of authority assembled. . . .

87. If any man smite out the eye or tooth of his manservant, or maidservant, or otherwise maim or much disfigure him, unless it be by mere casualty, he shall let them go free from his service. . . .

88. Servants that have served diligently and faithfully to the benefit of their masters seven years shall not be sent away empty. And if any have been unfaithful, negligent, or unprofitable in their service . . . they shall not be dismissed till they have made satisfaction. . . .

LIBERTIES OF FOREIGNERS AND STRANGERS

89. If any people of other nations professing the true Christian religion shall flee to us from the tyranny or oppression of their persecutors, or from famine, wars, or the like . . . they shall be entertained and succoured amongst us. . . .

90. If any ships or other vessels, be it friend or enemy, shall suffer shipwreck upon our coast, there shall be no violence or wrong offered to their persons or goods, but their persons shall be harboured and relieved and their goods preserved in safety until authority may be certified thereof. . . .

91. There shall never be any bond slavery, villeinage or captivity amongst us unless it be lawful captives taken in just wars and such strangers as willingly sell themselves or are sold to us. And these shall have all the liberties and Christian usages which the law of God established in Israel . . . doth morally require. This exempts none from servitude who shall be judged thereto by authority.

OF THE BRUTE CREATURE

92. No man shall exercise any tyranny or cruelty towards any brute creature which are usually kept for man's use.

93. If any man have occasion to lead or drive cattle from place to place that is far off so that they be weary or hungry, or fall sick or lame, it shall be lawful to rest or refresh them for competent time in any open place that is not corn, meadow, or enclosed for some peculiar use.

94. CAPITAL LAWS

1. If any man after legal conviction shall have or worship any other god but the Lord God, he shall be put to death.

2. If any man or woman be a witch (that is, hath or consulteth with a familiar spirit), they shall be put to death.

3. If any person shall blaspheme the name of God, the Father, Son, or Holy Ghost with direct, express, presumptuous, or high-handed blasphemy, or shall curse God in the like manner, he shall be put to death.

4. If any person commit any willful murder, which is manslaughter committed upon premeditated malice, hatred, or cruelty not in a man's necessary and just defense, nor by mere casualty against his will, he shall be put to death.

5. If any person slayeth another suddenly in his anger or cruelty of passion, he shall be put to death.

6. If any person shall slay another through guile, either by poisoning or other such devilish practice, he shall be put to death.

7. If any man or woman shall lie with any beast or brute creature by carnal copulation they shall surely be put to death and the beast shall be slain and buried and not eaten.

8. If any man lieth with mankind as he lieth with a woman, both of them have committed abomination; they both shall surely be put to death.

9. If any person committeth adultery with a married or espoused wife, the adulterer and adulteress shall surely be put to death.

10. If any man stealeth a man or mankind, he shall surely be put to death.

11. If any man rise up by false witness, wittingly and of purpose to take away any man's life, he shall be put to death.

12. If any man shall conspire and attempt any invasion, insurrection, or public rebellion against our commonwealth . . . he shall be put to death.

95. A DECLARATION OF THE LIBERTIES THE LORD JESUS HATH GIVEN TO THE CHURCHES

1. All the people of God within this jurisdiction who are not in a church way, and be orthodox in judgement and not scandalous in life, shall have full liberty to gather themselves into a church estate, provided they do it in a Christian way. . . .

2. Every church hath full liberty to exercise all the ordinances of God according to the rules of Scripture.

3. Every church hath free liberty of election and ordination of all their officers. . . .

4. Every church hath free liberty of admission, recommendation, dismission, and expulsion . . . of their officers and members upon due cause. . . .

5. No injunctions are to be put upon any church, church officers, or member in point of doctrine, worship, or discipline. . . .

6.-11. [Details of church jurisdiction and government.]

96.-98. [These 'liberties', though not in the 'exact form of laws or statutes', are to have the force of law until, after three years' trial, 'such of them as shall not be altered or repealed' shall be ratified as law.]

American Historical Documents, 1000–1904 ('Harvard Classics' series, ed. C. W. Eliot, xlii, 1910), pp. 70–89

8   Freedom for the Individual in Rhode Island, 1647

Rhode Island, of all the New England colonies, cherished toleration and the freedom of the individual most. Several towns were founded by miscellaneous groups of religious refugees who frequently quarreled among themselves. Finally, in 1647, Roger Williams, founder of the first town at Providence, succeeded in getting the several towns to agree upon a federation and laws designed to give the maximum liberty to the individual.

Forasmuch as we have received from our noble lords and honoured governors, and that by virtue of an ordinance of the Parliament of England, a free and absolute charter of civil incorporation, etc., we do jointly agree to incorporate ourselves, and so to remain a body politic by the authority thereof, and therefore do declare to own ourselves and one another to be members of the same body, and to have right to the freedom and privileges thereof by subscribing our names to these words, following:

We, whose names are hereunder written, do engage ourselves to the utmost of our estates and strength, to maintain the authority and to enjoy the liberty granted to us by our charter, in the extent of it according to the letter, and to maintain each other by the same authority, in his lawful right and liberty.

And now since our charter gives us power to govern ourselves and such other as come among us, and by such a form of civil government as by the voluntary consent, etc., shall be found most suitable to our estate and condition.

It is agreed, by this present assembly thus incorporate, and by this present act declared, that the form of government established in Providence Plantations is democratical; that is to say, a government held by the free and voluntary consent of all, or the greater part of the free inhabitants.

And now to the end that we may give, each to other (notwithstanding our different consciences, touching the truth as it is in Jesus, where-of, upon the point we all make mention), as good and hopeful assurance as we are able, touching each man's peaceable and quiet enjoyment of his lawful right and liberty, we do agree unto, and by the authority above said, enact, establish, and confirm these orders following.

TOUCHING LAWS

1. That no person in this colony shall be taken or imprisoned, or be disseized of his lands or liberties, or be exiled, or any other otherwise molested or destroyed, but by the lawful judgement of his peers, or by some known law, and according to the letter of it, ratified and confirmed by the major part of the General Assembly lawfully met and orderly managed.

2. That no person shall . . . presume to bear or execute any office that is not lawfully called to it and confirmed in it; nor . . . presume to do more or less than those that . . . did authorize him to do.

3. That no Assembly shall have power to constitute any laws for the binding of others, or to ordain officers for the execution thereof but such as are founded upon the charter and rightly derived from the General Assembly, lawfully met and orderly managed.

4. That no person be employed in any service for the public administration of justice and judgement upon offenders, or between man and man, without good encouragement, and due satisfaction from the public, either out of the common stock, or out of the stocks of those that have occasioned his service; that so those that are able to serve, may not be unwilling, and those that are able and willing, may not be disabled by being overburdened. . . .

And now, forasmuch as our charter gives us power to make such laws . . . as we, or the greater part of us shall, by free consent, agree unto, and yet does premise that those laws . . . so made shall be comformable to the laws of England, so far as the nature and constitution of our place will admit, . . . we do agree and by this present act determine to make such laws and constitutions so conformable, etc., or rather to make those laws ours, and better known among us; that is to say, such of them and so far as the nature and constitution of our place will admit.

TOUCHING THE COMMON LAW

It being the common right among common men, and is profitable either to direct or correct all, without exception; and it being true which that great doctor of the Gentiles once said, that the law is made or brought to light, not for a righteous man, who is a law unto himself, but for the lawless and disobedient in the general, . . . the end of which is, as is propounded, to preserve every man safe in his own person, name, and estate; we do agree to make, or rather to bring such laws to light for the direction or correction of such lawless persons, and for their memories sake to reduce them to these five general laws or heads, viz.:

1. Under that head of murdering fathers and mothers, being the highest and most unnatural, are comprehended those laws that concern high treason, petty treason, rebellion, misbehaviour, and their accessories.

2. Under the law for manslayers are comprehended those laws that concern self-murder, murder, homicide, misadventure, casual death, cutting out the tongue or eyes, witchcraft, burglary, robbery, burning of houses, forcible entries, rescues and escape, riots, routs and unlawful assemblies, batteries, assaults and threats and their accessories.

3. Under the law for whoremongers, and those that defile themselves with mankind, being the chief of that nature, are comprehended those laws that concern sodomy, buggery, rape, adultery, fornication, and their accessories.

4. Under the law for menstealers, being the chief of that nature, are comprehended those laws that concern theft of men, larceny, trespasses by men or beasts, fraudulent dealing by deceitful bargain, [etc.] . . . by forging or raising records, writs, . . . etc., and by using false weights and measures and their accessories.

5. Under the law for liars and perjured persons . . . are comprehended such as concern perjury itself, breach of covenant, slander, false witness-bearing, and their accessories.

And as necessary concomitants hereof, to prevent murder, theft, and perjury, we do jointly agree in this present Assembly to make or produce such laws as concern provision for the poor, so that the impotent shall be maintained and the able employed. And to prevent poverties it is agreed that such laws be made and produced as concerns the ordering of alehouses and taverns, drunkenness and unlawful gaming therein; and instead of such, to propagate archery, which is both man-like and profitable; and to prevent whoredom and those evils before mentioned, it is agreed by this present Assembly to constitute and establish some ordinance touching marriage, probate of wills, and intestates.

Records of the Colony of Rhode Island and Providence Plantations in New England (1856-1865), i.156-60

9   New York Seeks the Liberties of Other Englishmen, 1683

In 1664, the English under orders from the Duke of York, later James II, captured New Netherlands and renamed it New York. The Duke of York received the territory as a proprietary grant and could rule virtually with absolute authority. Dissatisfaction in the colony was such that, in 1683, he approved a charter of liberties and privileges establishing a legislative assembly. This compact he later rescinded after he became king, but finally, in 1691, granted another which included most of the provisions of 1683.

For the better establishing the government of this province of New York, and that justice and right may be equally done to all persons within the same:

Be it enacted by the Governor, Council, and Representatives now in General Assembly met and assembled, and by the authority of the same: that the supreme legislative authority under his Majesty and Royal Highness, James, duke of York, Albany, etc., lord proprietor of the said province, shall for ever be and reside in a Governor, Council, and the people met in General Assembly.

That the exercise of the chief magistracy and administration of the government over the said province shall be in the said Governor, assisted by a Council with whose advice and consent, or with at least four of them, he is to rule and govern the same according to the laws thereof.

[Provision in case of death or absence of the governor.]

That according to the usage, custom, and practice of the realm of England, a sessions of a General Assembly be held in this province once in three years at least.

That every freeholder within this province, and freeman in any corporation, shall have his free choice and vote in the electing of the representatives without any manner of constraint or imposition. And that in all elections the majority of voices shall carry it, and by freeholders is understood everyone who is so understood according to the laws of England.

[Number of representatives for each county specified.]

That all persons chosen and assembled in manner aforesaid, or the major part of them, shall be deemed and accounted the representatives of this province, which said representatives together with the governor and his Council, shall for ever be the supreme and only legislative power under his Royal Highness of the said province.

That the said representatives may appoint their own times of meeting during their sessions and may adjourn their house from time to time to such time as to them shall seem meet and convenient.

That the said representatives are the sole judges of the qualifications of their own members, and likewise of all undue elections, and may from time to time purge their house as they shall see occasion during the said sessions.

That no member of the General Assembly or their servants during the time of their sessions and while they shall be going to and returning from the said Assembly, shall be arrested, sued, imprisoned, or any ways molested or troubled. . . . That all bills agreed upon by the said representatives, or the major part of them, shall be presented to the governor and his Council for their approbation and consent; all and every which said bills so approved of, consented to by the governor and his Council, shall be esteemed and accounted the laws of the province, which said laws shall continue and remain of force until they shall be repealed by the authority aforesaid. . . .

That in all cases of death or removal of any of the said representatives, the governor shall issue out summons by writ to the respective towns . . . willing and requiring the freeholders of the same to elect others in their place and stead.

That no freeman shall be taken and imprisoned or be disseized of his freehold or liberty or free customs . . . or condemned but by the lawful judgement of his peers and by the law of this province. Justice nor right shall be neither sold, denied, or deferred to any man within this province.

That no aid, tax, tallage, assessment, custom, loan, benevolence, or imposition whatsoever shall be laid, assessed, imposed, or levied on any of his Majesty's subjects within this province or their estates, upon any manner of colour or pretence, but by the act and consent of the Governor, Council, and representatives of the people in General Assembly met and assembled.

That no man of what estate or condition soever shall be put out of his lands or tenements, nor taken, nor imprisoned, nor disherited, nor banished, nor any ways destroyed without being brought to answer by due course of law.

That a freeman shall not be amerced for a small fault, but after the manner of his fault, and for a great fault, after the greatness thereof, saving to him his freehold; and a husbandman saving to him his wainage, and a merchant likewise saving to him his merchandise. . . .

All trials shall be by the verdict of twelve men, and as near as may be, peers or equals; and of the neighbourhood and in the county, shire, or division where the fact shall arise or grow. . . .

That in all cases capital or criminal there shall be a grand inquest, who shall first present the offence, and then twelve men of the neighbourhood to try the offender, who after his plea to the indictment shall be allowed his reasonable challenges. That in all cases whatsoever bail by sufficient sureties shall be allowed and taken, unless for treason or felony plainly and specially expressed and mentioned in the warrant of commitment. . . .

That no freeman shall be compelled to receive any mariners or soldiers into his house and there suffer them to sojourn against their wills, provided always it be not in time of actual war within this province.

That no commissions for proceeding by martial law against any of his Majesty's subjects within this province shall issue forth to any person or persons whatsoever, lest by colour of them any of his Majesty's subjects be destroyed or put to death, except all such officers, persons, and soldiers in pay throughout the government.

That from henceforward no lands within this province shall be esteemed or accounted a chattel or personal estate, but an estate of inheritance, according to the custom and practice of his Majesty's realm of England.

That no court or courts within this province have or at any time hereafter shall have any jurisdiction, power, or authority to grant out any execution or other writ whereby any man's land may be sold or any other way disposed of without the owner's consent. . . .

That no estate of a feme covert shall be sold or conveyed but by deed, acknowledged by her in some court of record, the woman being secretly examined if she doth it freely without threats or compulsion of her husband.

That all wills in writing attested by two credible witnesses shall be of the same force to convey lands as other conveyances, being registered in the secretary's office within forty days after the testator's death.

That a widow after the death of her husband shall have her dower and shall and may tarry in the chief house of her husband forty days after the death of her husband, within which forty days her dower shall be assigned her, and for her dower shall be assigned unto her the third part of all the lands of her husband during coverture, except she were endowed of less before marriage.

That all lands and heritages within this province and dependencies shall be free from all fines and licences upon alienations, and from all heriots, wardships, liveries, primer seisins, year day and waste escheats and forfeitures upon the death of parents and ancestors, natural, unnatural, casual, or judicial, and that for ever; cases of high treason only excepted.

That no person or persons which profess faith in God by Jesus Christ shall at any time be any ways molested, punished, disquieted, or called in question for any difference in opinion or matter of religious concernment, who do not actually disturb the civil peace of the province. . . .

And whereas all the respective Christian churches now in practice within the city of New York, and the other places of this province, do appear to be privileged churches and have been so established and confirmed by the former authority of this government: be it hereby enacted by this General Assembly and by the authority thereof, that all the said respective Christian churches be hereby confirmed therein, and that they and every of them shall from henceforth for ever be held and reputed as privileged churches, and enjoy all their former freedoms of their religion in divine worship and church discipline; and that all former contracts made and agreed upon for the maintenances of the several ministers of the said churches, shall stand and continue in full force and virtue . . . provided also that all Christian churches that shall hereafter come and settle within this province shall have the same privileges.

The Colonial Laws of New York from the Year
1664 to the Revolution (1894), i.111-16

10   The Pennsylvania Charter of Privileges, 1701

The charter for the settlement of Pennsylvania was granted in 1681 to William Penn by Charles II, 'having regard to the memory and merits of his late father', Admiral Sir William Penn, who had won a naval victory against the Dutch. A 'frame of government' for the colony, drawn up in England by Penn and others in 1682, proved unwieldy in practice and was followed by two subsequent 'frames'. After many difficulties, including Penn's fall from royal favour under King William, the final Charter of Privileges was drafted by committee in 1701 and remained in effect until 1776.

William Penn, Proprietary and Governor of the province of Pennsylvania and territories thereunto belonging, to all to whom these presents shall come, sendeth greeting. Whereas King Charles the Second, by his letters patents under the Great Seal of England . . . was graciously pleased to give and grant unto me and my heirs and assigns forever this province of Pennsylvania. . . .

Know ye therefore that, for the further well-being and good government of the said province and territories, and in pursuance of the rights and powers before mentioned, I, the said William Penn, do declare, grant and confirm unto all the freemen, planters . . . and other inhabitants of this province and territories these following liberties. . . .

FIRST

Because no people can be truly happy, tho' under the greatest enjoyment of civil liberties, if abridged of the freedom of their consciences as to their religious profession and worship . . . I do hereby grant . . . that no person or persons inhabiting in this province or territories, who shall confess and acknowledge one almighty God, the Creator, Upholder, and Ruler of the world; and profess him or themselves obliged to live quietly under the civil government, shall be in any case molested or prejudiced, in his or their person or estate, because of his or their conscientious persuasion or practice; nor be compelled to frequent or maintain any religious worship . . . contrary to his or their mind; or to do or suffer any other act or thing contrary to their religious persuasion.

And that all persons who also profess to believe in Jesus Christ, the saviour of the world, shall be capable . . . to serve this government in any capacity, both legislatively and executively, he or they solemnly promising . . . allegiance to the King as sovereign, and fidelity to the Proprietary and Governor, and taking the attests as now established by the law made at Newcastle. . . .

II

For the well governing of this province and territories there shall be an assembly yearly chosen by the freemen thereof, to consist of four persons out of each county of most note for virtue, wisdom, and ability. . . . Which assembly shall have power to choose a speaker and other their officers; and shall be judges of the qualifications and elections of their own members; sit upon their own adjournments; appoint committees; prepare bills in order to pass into laws; impeach criminals, and redress grievances. And shall have all other powers and privileges of an assembly according to the rights of the freeborn subjects of England, and as is usual in any of the King's plantations in America. . . .

III

That the freemen in each respective county, at the time and place of meeting for electing their representatives to serve in assembly, may, as often as there shall be occasion, choose a double number of persons to present to the Governor for sheriffs and coroners, to serve for three years if so long they behave themselves well; out of which respective elections and presentments the Governor shall nominate and commissionate one for each of the said offices. . . .

And that the justices of the respective counties shall or may nominate and present to the Governor three persons, to serve for Clerk of the Peace for the said county when there is a vacancy. . . .

IV

[Gives the style and manner of recording of the laws.]

V

That all criminals shall have the same privileges of witnesses and counsel as their prosecutors.

VI

That no person or persons shall or may, at any time hereafter, be obliged to answer any complaint, matter, or thing whatsoever relating to property before the Governor and Council, or in any other place but in ordinary course of justice, unless appeals thereunto shall be hereafter by law appointed.

VII

That no person within this government shall be licensed by the Governor to keep an ordinary, tavern, or house of public entertainment but such who are first recommended to him under the hands of the justices of the respective counties, signed in open court. Which justices are and shall be hereby empowered to suppress and forbid any person keeping such public house as aforesaid, upon their misbehaviour, on such penalties as the law doth or shall direct. And to recommend others from time to time as they shall see occasion.

VIII

If any person, through temptation or melancholy, shall destroy himself, his estate, real and personal, shall notwithstanding descend to his wife and children, or relations, as if he had died a natural death. And if any person shall be destroyed or killed by casualty or accident there shall be no forfeiture to the Governor by reason thereof.

And no act, law, or ordinance whatsoever shall, at any time hereafter, be made or done to alter, change, or diminish the form or effect of this charter . . . without the consent of the Governor for the time being, and six parts of seven of the assembly met.

But because the happiness of mankind depends so much upon the enjoying of liberty of their consciences as aforesaid, I do hereby solemnly declare . . . that the first article of this charter relating to liberty of conscience . . . shall be kept and remain without any alteration, inviolably, forever.

And lastly I, the said William Penn, Proprietor and Governor of the province of Pennsylvania . . . do hereby solemnly declare . . . that neither I, my heirs or assigns, shall procure or do anything or things whereby the liberties of this charter . . . shall be infringed or broken. . . .

> *Votes and Proceedings of the House of Representatives of . . . Pennsylvania* [known as 'Votes of the Assembly'], I (1752), 2. Reprinted in *Amer. Col. Docs.* ed. Jensen, pp. 192-5

11   The Charter of Georgia, 1732

The 'Trustees for establishing the colony of Georgia in America' were a group of wealthy Englishmen of affairs persuaded to the enterprise by General James E. Oglethorpe, 'a gentleman of unblemished character, brave, generous, and humane'. The motives of Oglethorpe and the other trustees seem to have been the most public-spirited of any of the colonial proprietors. The new colony, named for George II, was to provide an outlet for England's overcrowded debtors' prisons and a buffer state between the Carolinas and the Spanish settlements to the south.

George the Second   [etc.] . . .

Whereas we are credibly informed that many of our poor subjects are, through misfortunes and want of employment, reduced to great necessity, insomuch as by their labour they are not able to provide a maintenance for themselves and families; and if they had means to defray their charges of passage and other expenses incident to new settlements, they would be glad to settle in any of our provinces in America where, by cultivating the lands at present waste and desolate, they might not only gain a comfortable subsistence for themselves and families, but also strengthen our colonies and increase the trade, navigation, and wealth of these our realms. And whereas our provinces in North America have been frequently ravaged by Indian enemies; more especially that of South Carolina which, in the late war, by the neighbouring savages was laid waste by fire and sword and great numbers of English inhabitants miserably massacred; and our loving subjects who now inhabit them, by reason of the smallness of their numbers, will, in case of a new war, be exposed to the late calamities, inasmuch as their whole southern frontier continueth unsettled and lieth open to the said savages.

And whereas we think it highly becoming our crown and royal dignity to protect all our loving subjects, be they never so distant from us. . . . And whereas we have been well assured that if we will be graciously pleased to erect and settle a corporation for the receiving, managing, and disposing of the contributions of our loving subjects, divers persons would be induced to contribute to the purposes aforesaid: Know ye therefore that we . . . grant that our right trusty and well beloved John, Lord Viscount Percival, of our kingdom of Ireland; our trusty and well beloved Edward Digby, George Carpenter, James Oglethorpe [etc.] . . . and such other persons as shall be elected in the manner hereinafter directed, be, and shall be, one body politic and corporate, in deed and in name, by the name of the Trustees for establishing the colony of Georgia in America. . . . And that they and their successors by that name shall and may forever hereafter be persons able and capable in the law to purchase . . . any manors . . . and other hereditaments whatsoever, lying and being in Great Britain or any part thereof . . . in fee and in perpetuity, not exceeding the yearly value of one thousand pounds. . . . And that they and their successors . . . be persons able, capable in the law, to purchase . . . any lands . . . lying and being in America . . . for the better settling and supporting and maintaining the said colony. . . . And we do further grant . . . that the said corporation . . . may from time to time, and at all times, meet about their affairs when and where they please and transact and carry on the business of the said corporation. And for the better execution of the purposes aforesaid, we do . . . give and grant to the said corporation and their successors that they . . . choose and elect such person or persons to be members of the said corporation as they shall think beneficial to the good designs of the said corporation. . . .

Our further will and pleasure is that no president of the said corporation shall have, take, or receive . . . any salary, fee, perquisite, benefit, or profit whatsoever for or by reason of his or their serving the said corporation. . . . And our will and pleasure is that the said hereinbefore appointed president, chairman, or common council-men, before he and they act respectively as such, shall severally take an oath for the faithful and due execution of their trust, to be administered to the president by the Chief Baron of our Court of Exchequer, for the time being. . . . And our will and pleasure is that all and every person and persons [who] shall have in his or their own name or names . . . any place, office, or employment of profit under the said corporation shall be incapable of being elected a member of the said corporation.. . .

And we do . . . grant unto the said corporation that they and their successors . . . shall have power from time to time . . . to authorize and appoint such persons as they shall think fit to take subscriptions and to gather and collect such moneys as shall be by any person or persons contributed for the purposes aforesaid. . . .

And we do hereby . . . ordain and direct that the said corporation every year lay an account in writing before the chancellor, or speaker, or commissioners for the custody of the great seal of Great Britain . . . of all moneys and effects by them received or expended for carrying on the good purposes aforesaid.

And we do hereby . . . give and grant unto the said corporation . . . full power and authority to constitute, ordain, and make such and so many by-laws . . . as to them . . . shall seem necessary and convenient for the well ordaining and governing of the said corporation. . . .

And for the greater ease and encouragement of our loving subjects, and such others as shall come to inhabit in our said colony, we do . . . ordain that forever hereafter there shall be a liberty of conscience allowed in the worship of God to all persons inhabiting, or which shall inhabit or be resident within, our said province. And that all such persons, except papists, shall have a free exercise of religion, so they be contented with the quiet and peaceable enjoyment of the same, not giving offence or scandal to the government.

And our further will and pleasure is . . . that it shall and may be lawful for the said common council . . . to distribute, convey, assign and set over such particular portions of lands . . . unto such our loving subjects, natural born, denizens, or others, that shall be willing to become our subjects and live under our allegiance in the said colony, upon such terms ... as the same may be lawfully granted and as to the said common council ... shall seem fit and proper. Provided always that no grants shall be made of any part of the said lands unto any person being a member of the said corporation; and that no person having any estate or interest, in law or equity, in any part of the said lands shall be capable of being a member of the said corporation. ...

And our further will and pleasure is that the said corporation and their successors do ... register or cause to be registered all such leases ... and improvements whatsoever as shall at any time hereafter be made by, or in the name of, the said corporation. ... And shall yearly send and transmit ... authentic accounts of such leases ... unto the auditor of the plantations ... to inspect and survey such of the said lands and premises as shall be demised, granted, and settled as aforesaid. Which said survey and inspection we do hereby declare to be intended to ascertain the quitrents which shall from time to time become due to us ... strictly enjoining and commanding that neither our or their surveyor, or any person whatsoever, under the pretext and colour of making the said survey or inspection, shall take, demand, or receive any gratuity, fee, or reward of or from any person or persons inhabiting in the said colony. ...

Every governor of the said province of Georgia, to be appointed by the common council of the said corporation ... shall be approved by us. ...

The governor and commander in chief of the province of South Carolina ... shall at all times hereafter have the chief command of the militia of our said province. ...

We ... do give and grant unto the said corporation ... full power and authority to import and export their goods at and from any port or ports that shall be appointed by us ... within the said province of Georgia for that purpose, without being obliged to touch at any other port in South Carolina.

And we do ... will and declare ... that from and after the determination of the said term of twenty-one years the governor of our said province of Georgia, and all officers civil and military within the same, shall from time to time be nominated and constituted and appointed by us, our heirs and successors. ...

Federal and State Constitutions, ed. Poore, i. 369–77

IV

RELIGION AND EDUCATION

1   The Founding of Harvard College, 1636

A tract published in London in 1643 bearing the title, *New Englands First Fruits*, served as propaganda for the Massachusetts Bay Colony. It contained a passage that described the founding of Harvard College in 1636 and listed the rules and curriculum.

New England's First Fruits: 2. In respect of the college, and the proceedings of learning therein.

After God had carried us safe to New England, and we had built our houses, provided necessaries for our livelihood, reared convenient places for God's worship, and settled the civil government, one of the next things we longed for and looked after was to advance learning and perpetuate it to posterity; dreading to leave an illiterate ministry to the churches, when our present ministers shall lie in the dust. And as we were thinking and consulting how to effect this great work, it pleased God to stir up the heart of one Mr. Harvard (a godly gentleman and a lover of learning, there living amongst us) to give the one half of his estate (it being in all about £1700) towards the erecting of a college, and all his library. After him, another gave £300; others after them cast in more, and the public hand of the State added the rest. The college was, by common consent, appointed to be at Cambridge (a place very pleasant and accommodate), and is called, according to the name of the first founder, Harvard College.

The edifice is very fair and comely within and without, having in it a spacious hall, where they daily meet at Commons, lectures, exercises, and a large library with some books to it, the gifts of divers of our friends; their chambers and studies also fitted for and possessed by the students, and all other rooms of office necessary and convenient, with all needful offices thereto belonging. And by the side of the college, a fair grammar school, for the training up of young scholars and fitting of them for academical learning, that still, as they are judged ripe, they may be received into the college of this school. Master Corlet is the master, who hath very well approved himself for his abilities, dexterity, and painfulness in teaching and education of the youth under him.

Over the college is Master Dunster placed as President, a learned, conscionable, and industrious man, who hath so trained up his pupils in the tongues and arts, and so seasoned them with the principles of divinity and Christianity, that we have, to our great comfort and, in truth, beyond our hopes, beheld their progress in learning and godliness also. The former of these hath appeared in their public declamations in Latin and Greek, and disputations logical and philosophical, which they have been wonted (besides their ordinary exercises in the college hall), in the audience of the magistrates, ministers, and other scholars, for the probation of their growth in learning, upon set days, constantly once every month, to make and uphold. The latter hath been manifested in sundry of them by the savory breathings of their spirits in their godly conversation. Insomuch that we are confident, if these early blossoms may be cherished and warmed with the influence of the friends of learning and lovers of this pious work, they will, by the help of God, come to happy maturity in a short time.

Over the college are twelve overseers chosen by the General Court. Six of them are of the magistrates, the other six of the ministers, who are to promote the best good of it; and, having a power of influence into all persons in it, are to see that every one be diligent and proficient in his proper place.

> [John Eliot], *New Englands First Fruits* (1643).
> Reprinted in S. E. Morison, *The Founding of
> Harvard College* (1935), Appen. D, pp. 432-3

2   Ill Effects of Book-Learning on Women, 1645

Seventeenth-century Puritans, like others in their time, were not convinced that women should meddle over-much with book-learning. This passage from John Winthrop's *Journal* indicates the point of view:

[April 13, 1645] Mr. Hopkins, the governor of Hartford upon Connecticut, came to Boston and brought his wife with him (a godly young woman, and of special parts), who was fallen into a sad infirmity: the loss of her understanding and reason; which had been growing upon her divers years by occasion of her giving herself wholly to reading and writing, and had written many books. Her husband, being very loving and tender of her, was loath to grieve her; but he saw his error, when it was too late. For if she had attended her household affairs, and such things as belong to women, and not gone out of her way and calling to meddle in such things as are proper for men, whose minds are stronger, etc., she had kept her wits, and might have improved them usefully and honorably in the place God had set her. He brought her to Boston, and left her with her brother, one Mr. Yale, a merchant, to try what means might be had here for her. But no help could be had.

> John Winthrop, *Journal*, published as *The History of New England*, ed. James Savage (1825-6). Reprinted, *Winthrop's Journal* (2 vols., 'Orig. Narr. Series'), ed. J. K. Hosmer (1908), ii.225

3   Provisions for Schools in Massachusetts, 1647

A law enacted by the General Court of Massachusetts Bay Colony on 11 November 1647 further strengthened the legal requirements for the education of children in that colony. A previous law enacted in 1642 had required parents to see that their children learned to read. Magistrates were required to apprentice orphans to masters who would teach them a trade as well as see that they learned to read.

It being one chief project of that old deluder, Satan, to keep men from the knowledge of the Scriptures, as in former times by keeping them in an unknown tongue, so in these latter times by persuading from the use of tongues, that so at least the true sense and meaning of the original might be clouded by false glosses of saint-seeming deceivers, that learning may not be buried in the grave of our fathers in the church and commonwealth, the Lord assisting our endeavours.

It is therefore ordered, that every township in this jurisdiction, after the Lord hath increased them to the number of fifty householders, shall then forthwith appoint one within their town to teach all such children as shall resort to him to write and read, whose wages shall be paid either by the parents or masters of such children, or by the inhabitants in general, by way of supply, as the major part of those that order the prudentials of the town shall appoint; provided those that send their children be not oppressed by paying much more than they can have them taught for in other towns; and it is further ordered that where any town shall increase to the number of 100 families or householders, they shall set up a grammar school, the master thereof being able to instruct youth so far as they may be fitted for the university, provided that if any town neglect the performance hereof above one year, that every such town shall pay £5 to the next school till they shall perform this order.

Records of . . . Massachusetts Bay, ed. N. B. Shurtleff (1853-4), ii. 203. Reprinted in *Amer. Col. Docs.*, ed. Jensen, pp. 560-1

4 A Puritan Argues against Toleration, 1647

The notion that the Puritans came to the New World in search of 'religious toleration' has been often refuted but the statement still appears in popular works. They came to find freedom from interference with their own particular form of worship and they themselves inveighed against toleration. A good example of this view is found in Nathaniel Ward, *The Simple Cobler of Aggawam* (1647).

. . . First, such as have given or taken any unfriendly reports of us New English, should do well to recollect themselves. We have been reputed a colluvies of wild opinionists, swarmed into a remote wilderness to find elbow-room for our fanatic doctrines and practices; I trust our diligence past, and constant sedulity against such persons and courses, will plead better things for us. I dare take upon me to be the herald of New England so far as to proclaim to the world, in the name of our colony, that all Familists, Antinomians, Anabaptists, and other enthusiasts, shall have free liberty to keep away from us, and such as will come, to be gone as fast as they can, the sooner the better.

Secondly, I dare aver, that God doth nowhere in his word tolerate Christian states to give tolerations to such adversaries of his truth, if they have power in their hands to suppress them.

Here is lately brought us an extract of a Magna Charta, so called, compiled between the subplanters of a West Indian island, whereof the first article of constipulation firmly provides free stable-room and litter for all kinds of consciences, be they never so dirty or jadish: making it actionable, yea, treasonable, to disturb any man in his religion or to discommend it, whatever it be. We are very sorry to see such professed profaneness in English professors, as industriously to lay their religious foundation on the ruin of true religion, which strictly binds every conscience to contend earnestly for the truth: to preserve unity of spirit, faith, and ordinances, to be all like minded, of one accord; every man to take his brother into his Christian care; to stand fast with one spirit, with one mind, striving together for the faith of the Gospel, and by no means to permit heresies or erroneous opinions. But God abhorring such loathsome beverages, hath in his righteous judgment blasted that enterprise, which might otherwise have prospered well, for aught I know. I presume their case is generally known ere this.

If the devil might have his free option I believe he would ask nothing else but liberty to enfranchise all other religions, and to embondage the true, nor should he need. It is much to be feared, that lax tolerations upon state pretences and planting necessities, will be the next subtle stratagem he will spread, to disstate the truth of God and supplant the peace of the churches. Tolerations in things tolerable, exquisitely drawn out by the lines of the Scripture, and pencil of the Spirit, are the sacred favours of truth, the due latitudes of love, the fair compartiments of Christian fraternity; but irregular dispensations, dealt forth by the facilities of men, are the frontiers of error, the redoubts of schism, the perilous irritaments of carnal enmity.

My heart hath naturally detested four things: The standing of the Apocrypha in the Bible; foreigners dwelling in my country, to crowd out native subjects into the corners of the earth; alchemized coins; tolerations of divers religions, or of one religion in segregant shapes. . . .

> Nathaniel Ward, *The Simple Cobler of Aggawam* (1647). Modern reprint by Lawrence C. Wroth (1937), pp. 2-4

5 Toleration in Maryland, 1649

Lord Baltimore planned to make the province of Maryland, of which he was Lord Proprietor, a haven for distressed Catholics. But he also wished to attract settlers of other faiths. To reassure them, he saw to it that the Maryland assembly on 21 April 1649 passed an Act of Toleration. When the Puritans for a time seized power in 1654 they repealed the Act, but it was restored when Baltimore regained control.

Forasmuch as in a well-governed and Christian commonwealth matters concerning religion and the honour of God ought in the first place to be taken into serious consideration, and endeavoured to be settled: Be it therefore . . . enacted . . . that whatsoever person or persons within this province . . . shall from henceforth blaspheme God . . . or shall deny our Saviour Jesus Christ to be the son of God, or shall deny the holy Trinity . . . shall be punished with death and confiscation or forfeiture of all his or her lands. . . .

. . . And whereas the enforcing of the conscience in matters of religion hath frequently fallen out to be of dangerous consequence in those commonwealths where it hath been practised, and for the more quiet and peaceable government of this province and the better to preserve mutual love and amity amongst the inhabitants thereof: Be it therefore . . . enacted . . . that no person or persons whatsoever within this province . . . professing to believe in Jesus Christ shall from henceforth be any ways troubled, molested, or discountenanced for, or in respect of, his or her religion, nor in the free exercise thereof within this province . . .; nor any way compelled to the belief or exercise of any other religion against his or her consent, so as they be not unfaithful to the Lord Proprietary, or molest or conspire against the civil government established, or to be established, in this province under him or his heirs. And that all & every person and persons that shall presume contrary to this Act and the true intent and meaning thereof, directly or indirectly, either in person or estate, willfully to wrong, disturb, trouble, or molest any person whatsoever within this province professing to believe in Jesus Christ, for or in respect of his or her religion or the free exercise thereof within this province, other than is provided for in this Act, that such person or persons so offending shall be compelled to pay treble damages to the party so wronged or molested, and for every such offence shall also forfeit 20s. sterling in money or the value thereof. . . . Or, if the parties so offending as aforesaid shall refuse or be unable to recompense the party so wronged, or to satisfy such fine or forfeiture, then such offender shall be severely punished by public whipping & imprisonment during the pleasure of the Lord Proprietary, or his Lieutenant or chief governor of this province for the time being, without bail or mainprize. . . .

> *The Archives of Maryland*, ed. W. H. Browne (1883-1912), i. 244ff., reprinted in *Documents of American History*, ed. H. S. Commager (1940), pp. 31-2

6 A Difference between Liberty and Licence, 1655

Roger Williams, founder of the colony of Rhode Island, consistently advocated toleration and freedom of conscience, but he was careful to point out that utter lack of restraint would lead to anarchy. In a letter addressed to the town of Providence he explains his views.

To the Town of Providence.

[Providence, January 1655.]

That ever I should speak or write a tittle that tends to such an infinite liberty of conscience, is a mistake, and which I have ever disclaimed and abhorred. To prevent such mistakes, I shall at present only propose this case: There goes many a ship to sea, with many hundred souls in one ship, whose weal and woe is common, and is a true picture of a commonwealth, or a human combination or society. It hath fallen out sometimes, that both papists and protestants, Jews and Turks, may be embarked in one ship; upon which supposal I affirm that all the liberty of conscience that ever I pleaded for, turns upon these two hinges – that none of the papists, protestants, Jews, or Turks be forced to come to the ship's prayers or worship, nor compelled from their own particular prayers or worship, if they practice any. I further add, that I never denied that, notwithstanding this liberty, the commander of this ship ought to command the ship's course, yea, and also command that justice, peace, and sobriety be kept and practiced, both among the seamen and all the passengers. If any of the seamen refuse to perform their services, or passengers to pay their freight; if any refuse to help, in person or purse, towards the common charges or defence; if any refuse to obey the common laws and orders of the ship, concerning their common peace or preservation; if any shall mutiny and rise up against their commanders and officers; if any should preach or write that there ought to be no commanders or officers, because all are equal in Christ, therefore no masters nor officers, no laws nor orders, nor corrections nor punishments; – I say, I never denied but in such cases, whatever is pretended, the commander or commanders may judge, resist, compel, and punish such transgressors, according to their deserts and merits. This if seriously and honestly minded, may, if it so please the Father of lights, let in some light to such as willingly shut not their eyes.

I remain studious of your common peace and liberty.

ROGER WILLIAMS.
The Letters of Roger Williams, ed. J. R. Bartlett (*Publications of the Narragansett Club*, vi, 1874), pp. 278-9. Reprinted in *American Literature*, eds. C. Bode, L. Howard, L. B. Wright (1966), i.72

7   Persecution of Quakers Justified, 1659

Massachusetts Bay Colony passed laws against heresy and dissent and did its best to stamp out any deviation from orthodoxy. Members of the Society of Friends (Quakers) excited the particular ire of the authorities, not only among New England Puritans but elsewhere in the colonies. Rhode Island was the only New England colony that tolerated them. Massachusetts Bay was particularly severe on Quakers. In 1659, William Robinson, Marmaduke Stevenson, and Mary Dyer, Quakers, were arrested. Mary Dyer was allowed to leave the colony but later returned and was hanged. Robinson and Stevenson, while awaiting execution, wrote a defence of themselves, which the General Court attempted to answer in the statement given below.

Although the justice of our proceedings against William Robinson, Marmaduke Stevenson, and Mary Dyer, supported by the authority of this court, the laws of the country, and the law of God, may rather persuade us to expect encouragement and commendation from all prudent and pious men, than convince us of any necessity to apologize for the same, yet for as much as men of weaker parts, out of pity and commiseration (a commendable and Christian virtue, yet easily abused, and susceptible of sinister and dangerous impressions) for want of full information, may be less satisfied, and men of perverser principles may take occasion hereby to calumniate us, and render us as bloody persecutors; to satisfy the one, and stop the mouths of the other, we thought it requisite to declare: That about three years since divers persons, professing themselves Quakers (of whose pernicious opinions and practices we had received intelligence from good hands, from Barbados to England) arrived at Boston, whose persons were only secured to be sent away by the first opportunity, without censure or punishment, although their professed tenets, turbulent and contemptuous behaviour to authority would have justified a severer animadversion;' yet the prudence of this court was exercised only in making provision to secure the peace and order here established, against their attempts, whose design (we were well assured of by our own experience, as well as by the example of their predecessors in Münster) was to undermine and ruin the same; and accordingly a law was made and published prohibiting all masters of ships to bring any Quakers into this jurisdiction, and themselves from coming in, on penalty of the house of correction, till they could be sent away. Notwithstanding which, by a back door they found entrance, and the penalty inflicted on themselves, proving insufficient to restrain their impudent and insolent obtrusions, was increased by the loss of the ears of those that offended the second time, which also being too weak a defence against their impetuous frantic fury, necessitated us to endeavour our security, and upon serious consideration, after the former experiments, by their incessant assaults, a law was made, that such persons should be banished, on pain of death, according to the example of England in their provision against Jesuits, which sentence being regularly pronounced at the last Court of Assistants against the parties above named, and they either returning, or continuing presumptuously in this jurisdiction, after the time limited, were apprehended, and owning themselves to be the persons banished, were sentenced (by the court) to death, according the law aforesaid, which hath been executed upon two of them. Mary Dyer, upon the petition of her son and the mercy and clemency of this court, had liberty to depart within two days, which she hath accepted of. The consideration of our gradual proceeding will vindicate us from the clamorous accusations of severity; our own just and necessary defence, calling upon us (other means failing) to offer the point which these persons have violently and wilfully rushed upon, and thereby become *felons de se*, which might it have been prevented, and the sovereign law *salus populi* been preserved, our former proceedings, as well as the sparing of Mary Dyer, upon an inconsiderable intercession, will manifestly evince, we desire their lives absent, rather than their death present.

Massachusetts Historical Society *Proceedings*, xlii (1908-9), reprinted in *Amer. Col. Docs.*, ed. Jensen, pp. 532-3

8   Quakers Oppose Slavery, 1688

The Society of Friends as a group opposed slavery. At a meeting at Germantown in 1688, a body of Quakers passed a resolution expressing their opposition to the sale of men into bondage.

These are the reasons why we are against the traffic of mens-body as follows ... Now, though they are black, we cannot conceive there is more liberty to have them slaves as it is to have other white ones. There is a saying that we shall do to all men like as we will be done ourselves; making no difference of what generation, descent or colour they are. And those who steal or rob men, and those who buy or purchase them, are they not all alike? Here is liberty of conscience, which is right and reasonable; here ought to be likewise liberty of the body, except of evil-doers, which is another case. But to bring men hither, or to rob and sell them against their will, we stand against. In Europe there are many oppressed for conscience sake; and here there are those oppressed which are of a black colour. . . . This makes an ill report in all those countries of Europe, where they hear of that the Quakers do here handle men like they handle there the cattle. And for that reason some have no mind or inclination to come hither. . . . Therefore, we contradict, and are against this traffic of mens-body. And we who profess that it is not lawful to steal, must, likewise, avoid to purchase such things as are stolen, but rather help to stop this robbing and stealing, if possible. And such men ought to be delivered out of the hands of the robbers and set free as well as in Europe. Then is Pennsylvania to have a good report; instead, it has now a bad one for this sake in other countries; especially whereas the Europeans are desirous to know in what manner *the Quakers* do rule in *their* province; and most of them do look upon us with an envious eye. But if this is done well, what shall we say is done evil?

If once these slaves (which they say are so wicked and stubborn men), should join themselves – fight for their freedom, and handle their master and mistresses as they did handle them before; will these masters and mistresses take the sword at hand and war against these poor slaves, like we are able to believe, some will not refuse to do? Or, have these Negroes not as much right to fight for their freedom as you have to keep them slaves?

Now, consider well this thing, if it is good or bad. And in case you find it to be good to handle these blacks in that manner, we desire and require you hereby lovingly that you may inform us herein, which at this time never was done, viz., that Christians have liberty to do so. To the end we shall be satisfied on this point, and satisfy likewise our good friends and acquaintances in our native country, to whom it is a terror or fearful thing, that men should be handled so in Pennsylvania. . . .

Pennsylvania Magazine of History and Biography,
iv (1880), pp. 28-30

9 Witchcraft Hysteria in Salem, 1692

The witchcraft hysteria that swept Salem and Andover, Massachusetts, in 1692-3 was a phenomenon of the times not peculiar to Puritan New England.

It had followed like an epidemic in the wake of the religious wars through Europe via England to the American colonies. The hysteria that erupted in Salem coincided with the appointment of a new governor of the colony, Sir William Phips, who at first condoned the prosecutions. Becoming alarmed at the spread of the contagion, Phips appealed to the celebrated Boston clergyman, Cotton Mather, for moral support. The result was Mather's book entitled *The Wonders of the Invisible World, Being an Account of the Tryals of Several Witches Lately Executed in New-England* (Boston, 1692; London, 1693).

. . . It may cast some light upon the dark things now in America if we just give a glance upon the like things lately happening in Europe. We may see the witchcrafts here most exactly resemble the witchcrafts there. And we may learn what sort of devils do trouble the world. . . .

THE TRIAL OF BRIDGET BISHOP, ALIAS
Oliver, at the Court of Oyer and Terminer,
held at Salem June 2, 1692

She was indicted for bewitching of several persons in the neighbourhood, the indictment being drawn up according to the form in such cases usual. And pleading *Not Guilty*, there were brought in several persons who had long undergone many kinds of miseries, which were preternaturally inflicted and generally ascribed unto an horrible witchcraft. There was little occasion to prove the witchcraft, it being evident and notorious to all beholders.

Now to fix the witchcraft on the prisoner at the bar, the first thing used was the testimony of the bewitched. Whereof several testified that the *shape* of the prisoner did oftentimes very grievously pinch them, choke them, bite them, and afflict them, urging them to write their names in a book which the said spectre called *Ours*. One of them did further testify that it was the shape of this prisoner, with another, which one day took her from her wheel and, carrying her to the riverside, threatened there to drown her if she did not sign to the book mentioned, which yet she refused. . . .

2. It was testified that at the examination of the prisoner before the magistrates the bewitched were extremely tortured. If she did but cast her eyes on them they were presently struck down, and this in such a manner as there could be no collusion in the business. But upon the touch of her hand upon them, when they lay in their swoons, they would immediately revive; and not upon the touch of anyone's else.

Moreover, upon some special actions of her body, as the shaking of her head or the turning of her eyes, they presently and painfully fell into the like postures. . . .

3. There was testimony likewise brought in that a man striking once at the place where a bewitched person said the shape of this Bishop stood, the bewitched cried out that he had tore her coat, in the place then particularly specified. And the woman's coat was found to be torn in that very place.

5. To render it further unquestionable that the prisoner at the bar was the person truly charged in this witchcraft, there were produced many evidences of other witchcrafts by her perpetrated. For instance, John Cook testified that about five or six years ago, one morning about sunrise, he was in his chamber assaulted by the shape of this prisoner, which looked on him, grinned at him, and very much hurt him with a blow on the side of the head; and that on the same day about noon the same shape walked in the room where he was and an apple strangely flew out of his hand into the lap of his mother, six or eight foot from him. . . .

12. To crown all, John Bly and William Bly testified that, being employed by Bridget Bishop to help to take down the cellar wall of the old house wherein she formerly lived, they did in holes of the said old wall find several poppets, make up of rags and hogs' bristles, with headless pins in them, the points being outward; whereof she could now give no account unto the Court that was reasonable or tolerable. . . .

14. There was one very strange thing more, with which the Court was newly entertained. As this woman was under a guard, passing by the great and spacious meeting-house of Salem, she gave a look towards the house. And immediately a demon, invisibly entering the meeting-house, tore down a part of it; so that, tho' there was no person to be seen there, yet the people, at the noise running in, found a board, which was strongly fastened with several nails, transported unto another quarter of the house.

Mather, *Wonders of the Invisible World* (London, 1693), reprinted in *Cotton Mather On Witchcraft* ([1950?]), pp. 92, 106-13

10   A College Founded in Virginia, 1693

The College of William and Mary, in Williamsburg, Virginia, founded by charter dated 1693, was the second institution of higher learning established in the colonies. Robert Beverley, who wrote a history of the colony published in 1705, gives a brief statement about its beginnings.

During that gentleman's presidency [Col. Nathaniel Bacon's], which began *Anno* 1689, the project of a college was first agreed upon. The contrivers drew up their scheme and presented it to the president and council. This was by them approved, and referred to the next assembly. But Col. Bacon's administration being very short and no assembly called all the while, this pious design could proceed no further.

Anno 1690. Francis Nicholson, Esq., being appointed lieutenant-governor under the Lord Effingham, arrived there. This gentleman's business was to fix himself in my lord's place, and recommend himself to the supreme government. For that end, he studied popularity, discoursing freely of country improvements. He made his court to the people by instituting Olympic games, and giving prizes to all those that should excel in the exercises of riding, running, shooting, wrestling and backsword. When the design of a college was communicated to him, he foresaw what interest it might create him with the bishops in England, and therefore promised it all imaginable encouragement. The first thing desired of him in its behalf was the calling of an assembly; but this he would by no means agree to. . . .

When that could not be obtained, then they proposed that a subscription might pass through the colony to try the humour of the people in general, and see what voluntary contributions they could get towards it. This he granted, and he himself, together with the Council, set a generous example to the other gentlemen of the country, so that the subscriptions at last amounted to about two thousand five hundred pounds, in which sum is included the generous benevolences of several merchants of London.

Anno 1691, an assembly being called, this design was moved to them, and they espoused it heartily; and soon after made an address to King William and Queen Mary in its behalf, and sent the Reverend Mr. James Blair their agent to England, to solicit their Majesties' charter for it.

It was proposed that three things should be taught in this college, viz., languages, divinity, and natural philosophy.

They appointed a certain number of professors, and their salaries.

And they formed rules for the continuation and good government thereof to perpetuity. . . .

Their Majesties were well pleased with that pious design of the plantation, and granted a charter, according to their desire; in obtaining which the address and assiduity of Mr. Blair, their agent, was highly to be admired.

Their Majesties were graciously pleased to give near two thousand pounds sterling, the balance due upon the account of quit-rents, towards the founding the college; and towards the endowing of it, they allowed twenty thousand acres of choice land, together with the revenue arising by the penny per pound, on tobacco exported from Virginia and Maryland to the other plantations.

It was a great satisfaction to the archbishops and bishops to see such a nursery of religion founded in that new world; especially for that it was begun in an Episcopal way, and carried on wholly by zealous conformists to the Church of England. . . .

Robert Beverley, *The History and Present State of Virginia* (1705), ed. L. B. Wright (1947), pp. 97-9

11   William Penn on Education, 1693

William Penn believed in adapting schools to the practical needs of the day rather than in following classic patterns of education. He indicates his views in the following passage:

We are in pain to make them [the youth of his day] scholars but not men, to talk rather than to know, which is true canting. . . . We press their memory too soon, and puzzle, strain, and load them with words and rules to know grammar and rhetoric, and a strange tongue or two that is ten to one may never be useful to them, leaving their natural genius to mechanical, physical, or natural knowledge uncultivated and neglected. . . . To be sure languages are not to be despised or neglected; but things are still to be preferred. . . . It were happy if we studied nature more in natural things, and acted according to nature, whose rules are few, plain, and most reasonable. . . . It is pity, therefore, that books have not been composed for youth by some curious and careful naturalists, and also mechanics, in the Latin tongue, to be used in schools, that they might learn things with words: things obvious and familiar to them, and which would make the tongue easier to be obtained by them.

> From [William Penn], *Some Fruits of Solitude* (1693), reprinted in J. P. Wickersham, *A History of Education in Pennsylvania* (1886), pp. 35-6

12   Franklin's Plan for a Well-Rounded Education, 1749

Benjamin Franklin, a man of many ideas in a variety of fields, printed a proposal in 1749 that led to the establishment in 1751 of a secular school, the Academy of Philadelphia. This academy illustrates the practical point of view not only of Franklin but of the Quakers of Pennsylvania.

ADVERTISEMENT TO THE READER

It has long been regretted as a misfortune to the youth of this province that we have no academy in which they might receive the accomplishments of a regular education. The following paper of hints towards forming a plan for that purpose is so far approved by some public spirited gentlemen to whom it has been privately communicated, that they have directed a number of copies to be made by the press and properly distributed, in order to obtain the sentiments and advice of men of learning, understanding, and experience in these matters; and have determined to use their interest and best endeavours to have the scheme when completed carried gradually into execution; in which they have reason to believe they shall have the hearty concurrence and assistance of many who are well-wishers to their country. Those who incline to favour the design with their advice either as to the parts of learning to be taught, the order of study, the method of teaching, the economy of the school, or any other matter of importance to the success of the undertaking, are desired to communicate their sentiments as soon as may be, by letter directed to B. Franklin, Printer, in Philadelphia.

PROPOSALS

... That we may obtain the advantages arising from an increase of knowledge, and prevent as much as may be the mischievous consequences that would attend a general ignorance among us, the following hints are offered towards forming a plan for the education of the youth of Pennsylvania, viz:

It is proposed that some persons of leisure and public spirit apply for a charter by which they may be incorporated, with power to erect an academy for the education of youth, to govern the same, provide masters, make rules, receive donations, purchase lands, etc., and to add to their number from time to time such other persons as they shall judge suitable.

That the members of the corporation make it their pleasure, and in some degree their business, to visit the academy often....

That a house be provided for the academy, if not in the town, not many miles from it; the situation high and dry, and if it may be, not far from a river, having a garden, orchard, meadow, and a field or two.

That the house be furnished with a library (if in the country; if in the town, the town libraries may serve) with maps of all countries, globes, some mathematical instruments, an apparatus for experiments in natural philosophy, and for mechanics; prints of all kinds, prospects, buildings, machines, etc.

That the rector be a man of good understanding, good morals, diligent and patient, learned in the languages and sciences, and a correct pure speaker and writer of the English tongue; to have such tutors under him as shall be necessary.

That the boarding scholars diet together, plainly, temperately, and frugally.

That to keep them in health, and to strengthen and render active their bodies, they be frequently exercised in running, leaping, wrestling, and swimming, etc.

That they have peculiar habits to distinguish them from other youth if the academy be in or near the town; for this, among other reasons, that their behaviour may be the better observed.

As to their studies, it would be well if they could be taught everything that is useful, and everything that is ornamental; but Art is long, and their time is short. It is therefore proposed that they learn those things that are likely to be most useful and most ornamental, regard being had to the several professions for which they are intended.

All should be taught to write a fair hand, and swift, as that is useful to all. And with it may be learnt something of drawing, by imitation of prints, and some of the first principles of perspective.

Arithmetic, accounts, and some of the first principles of geometry and astronomy.

The English language might be taught by grammar in which some of our best writers, as Tillotson, Addison, Pope, Algernon Sidney, Cato's Letters, etc., should be classics; the styles principally to be cultivated being the clear and the concise. Reading should also be taught, and pronouncing, properly, distinctly, emphatically; not with an even tone, which underdoes, nor a theatrical, which overdoes Nature.

To form their style they should be put on writing letters to each other, making abstracts of what they read; or writing the same things in their own words; telling or writing stories lately read in their own expressions. All to be revised and corrected by the tutor, who should give his reasons and explain the force and import of words, etc.

To form their pronunciation, they may be put on making declamations, repeating speeches, delivering orations, etc.; the tutor assisting at the rehearsals, teaching, advising, correcting their accent, etc.

But if history be made a constant part of their reading, such as the translations of the Greek and Roman historians, and the modern histories of ancient Greece and Rome, etc., may not almost all kinds of useful knowledge be that way introduced to advantage, and with pleasure to the student? As

Geography, by reading with maps, and being required to point out the places where the greatest actions were done, to give their old and new names, with the bounds, situation, extent of the countries concerned, etc.

Chronology, by the help of Helvicus or some other writer of the kind, who will enable them to tell when those events happened; what princes were contemporaries, what states or famous men flourished about that time, etc. The several principal epochs to be first well fixed in their memories.

Ancient customs, religious and civil, being frequently mentioned in history, will give occasion for explaining them; in which the prints of medals, basso-relievos, and ancient monuments will greatly assist.

Morality, by descanting and making continual observations on the causes of the rise or fall of any man's character, fortune, power, etc., mentioned in history; the advantages of temperance, order, frugality, industry, perseverance, etc., etc. Indeed the general natural tendency of reading good history must be to fix in the minds of youth deep impressions of the beauty and usefulness of virtue of all kinds, public spirit, fortitude, etc.

History will show the wonderful effects of oratory in governing, turning and leading great bodies of mankind, armies, cities, nations. . . .

[Long passage on the value of history is omitted.]

With the history of men, times, and nations, should be read at proper hours or days some of the best histories of nature, which would not only be delightful to youth, and furnish them with matter for their letters etc., as well as other history, but afterwards of great use to them, whether they are merchants, handicrafts, or divines; enabling the first the better to understand many commodities, drugs, etc.; the second to improve his trade or handicraft by new mixtures, materials, etc., and the last to adorn his discourses by beautiful comparisons, and strengthen them by new proofs of divine providence. The conversation of all will be improved by it as occasions frequently occur of making natural observations which are instructive, agreeable, and entertaining in almost all companies. Natural history will also afford opportunities of introducing many observations relating to the preservation of health, which may be afterwards of great use. Arbuthnot on air and aliment, Sanctorius on perspiration, Lemery on foods, and some others may now be read, and a very little explanation will make them sufficiently intelligible to youth.

While they are reading natural history, might not a little gardening, planting, grafting, inoculating, etc., be taught and practised, and now and then excursions made to the neighbouring plantations of the best farmers, their methods observed and reasoned upon for the information of youth? The improvement of agriculture being useful to all, and skill in it no disparagement to any.

The history of commerce, of the invention of arts, rise of manufactures, progress of trade, change of its seats, with the reasons, causes, etc., may also be made entertaining to youth, and will be useful to all. And this, with the accounts in other history of the prodigious force and effect of engines and machines used in war, will naturally introduce a desire to be instructed in mechanics, and to be informed of the principles of that art by which weak men perform such wonders, labour is saved, manufactures expedited, etc. This will be the time to show them prints of ancient and modern machines, to explain them, to let them be copied, and to give lectures in mechanical philosophy.

With the whole should be constantly inculcated and cultivated that benignity of mind which shows itself in searching for and seizing every opportunity to serve and to oblige, and is the foundation of what is called good breeding, highly useful to the possessor, and most agreeable to all.

The idea of what is true merit should also be often presented to youth, explained and impressed on their minds, as consisting in an inclination joined with an ability to serve mankind, one's country, friends and family, which ability is (with the blessing of God) to be acquired or greatly increased by true learning, and should indeed be the great aim and the end of all learning.

> Reprinted in *The Writings of Benjamin Franklin*, ed. A. H. Smyth (1905-7), ii.386-96

13   Diversity of Religions in Pennsylvania, 1750-1754

William Penn, himself a Quaker, sought to make his proprietary colony of Pennsylvania a refuge where Europeans persecuted for their religion could find safety. How well he succeeded is indicated in a description by Gottlieb Mittelberger, a German minister, who made an extensive visit to Pennsylvania beginning in 1750. He found it hard to understand the complete freedom of Pennsylvania and regarded the lack of order in religion with distaste.

Coming to speak of Pennsylvania again, that colony possesses great liberties above all other English colonies, inasmuch as all religious sects are tolerated there. We find there Lutherans, Reformed, Catholics, Quakers, Mennonists or Anabaptists, Herrnhuters or Moravian Brethren, Pietists, Seventh Day Baptists, Dunkers, Presbyterians, Newborn, Freemasons, Separatists, Freethinkers, Jews, Mohammedans,

Pagans, Negroes, and Indians. The Evangelicals and Reformed, how-ever, are in the majority. But there are many hundred unbaptized souls there that do not even wish to be baptized. Many pray neither in the morning nor in the evening, neither before nor after meals. No de-votional book, not to speak of a Bible, will be found with such people. In one house and one family, four, five, and even six sects may be found. . . .

The preachers throughout Pennsylvania have no power to punish any-one, or to compel anyone to go to church; nor has anyone a right to dictate to the other, because they are not supported by any *Consistorio*. Most preachers are hired by the year like the cowherds in Germany; and if one does not preach to their liking, he must expect to be served with a notice that his services will no longer be required. It is, therefore, very difficult to be a conscientious preacher, especially as they have to hear and suffer much from so many hostile and often wicked sects. The most exemplary preachers are often reviled, insulted, and scoffed at like the Jews, by the young and old, especially in the country. I would, therefore, rather perform the meanest herdsman's duties in Germany than be a preacher in Pennsylvania. Such unheard of rudeness and wickedness spring from the excessive liberties of the land, and from the blind zeal of the many sects. To many a one's soul and body, liberty in Pennsylvania is more hurtful than useful. There is a saying in that country: Pennsylvania is the heaven of the farmers, the paradise of the mechanics, and the hell of the officials and preachers.

Gottlieb Mittelberger, *Journey to Pennsylvania in the Year 1750 and Return to Germany in the Year 1754*, ed. and tr. C. T. Eben (1898), pp. 54-5, 61-3

V

ECONOMIC DEVELOPMENT

1 Navigation Act of 1660

The first of a series of Acts of Trade and Navigation relating to the colonies was enacted by the Commonwealth Parliament in 1650. The Act of 1660 made some of the provisions of the earlier acts more specific. Essentially the Acts of Trade and Navigation were designed to further the mercantilist aim of a closed empire in which the colonies would ship raw products only to the mother country in English or colonial ships.

For the increase of shipping and encouragement of the navigation of this nation wherein, under the good providence and protection of God, the wealth, safety, and strength of this kingdom is so much concerned; (2) be it enacted by the king's most excellent Majesty, and by the Lords and Commons in this present Parliament assembled, and by the authority thereof, that from and after the first day of December, one thousand six hundred and sixty, and from thence forward, no goods or commodities whatsoever shall be imported into or exported out of any lands, islands, plantations, or territories to his Majesty belonging or in his possession, or which may hereafter belong unto or be in the possession of his Majesty, his heirs, and successors, in Asia, Africa, or America, in any other ship or ships, vessel or vessels whatsoever, but in such ships or vessels as do truly and without fraud belong only to the people of England or Ireland, dominion of Wales or town of Berwick upon Tweed, or are of the build of and belonging to any the said lands, islands, plantations, or territories, as the proprietors and right owners thereof, and whereof the master and three fourths of the mariners at least are English. . . .

II. And be it enacted, that no alien or person not born within the allegiance of our sovereign lord the king, his heirs and successors, or naturalized, or made a free denizen, shall from and after the first day of February, which will be in the year of our Lord one thousand six hundred sixty-one, exercise the trade or occupation of a merchant or factor in any the said places; (2) upon pain of the forfeiture and loss of all his goods and chattels, or which are in his possession; one third to his Majesty, his heirs and successors; one third to the governor of the plantation where such person shall so offend; and the other third to him or them that shall inform or sue for the same in any of his Majesty's courts in the plantation where such offence shall be committed. . . .

III. And it is further enacted by the authority aforesaid, that no goods or commodities whatsoever, of the growth, production or manu-facture of Africa, Asia, or America, or of any part thereof, or which are described or laid down in the usual maps or cards of those places, be imported into England, Ireland, or Wales, islands of Guernsey and Jersey, or town of Berwick upon Tweed, in any other ship or ships, vessel or vessels whatsoever, but in such as do truly and without fraud belong only to the people of England or Ireland, dominion of Wales, or town of Berwick upon Tweed, or of the lands, islands, plantations or territories in Asia, Africa, or America, to his Majesty belonging, as the proprietors and right owners thereof, and whereof the master and three fourths at least of the mariners are English; (2) under the penalty of the forfeiture of all such goods and commodities, and of the ship or vessel in which they were imported, with all her guns, tackle, furniture, ammunition, and apparel; one moiety to his Majesty, his heirs and successors; and the other moiety to him or them who shall seize, in-form or sue for the same in any court of record, by bill, information, plaint or other action, wherein no essoin, protection or wager of law shall be allowed. . . .

XVIII. And it is further enacted by the authority aforesaid, that from and after the first day of April, which shall be in the year of our Lord one thousand six hundred sixty-one, no sugars, tobacco, cotton-wool, indigoes, ginger, fustic, or other dyeing wood, of the growth, pro-duction, or manufacture of any English plantations in America, Asia, or Africa, shall be shipped, carried, conveyed, or transported from any of the said English plantations to any land, island, territory, dominion, port, or place whatsoever, other than to such other English plantations as do belong to his Majesty, his heirs and successors, or to the kingdom of England or Ireland, or principality of Wales, or town of Berwick upon Tweed, there to be laid on shore; (2) under the penalty of the forfeiture of the said goods, or the full value thereof, as also of the ship, with all her guns, tackle, apparel, ammunition, and furniture; the one moiety to the king's Majesty, his heirs and successors, and the other moiety to him or them that shall seize, inform, or sue for the same in any court of record, by bill, plaint, or information, wherein no essoin, protection, or wager of law shall be allowed.

XIX. And be it further enacted by the authority aforesaid, that for every ship or vessel, which from and after the five and twentieth day of December in the year of our Lord one thousand six hundred and sixty shall set sail out of or from England, Ireland, Wales, or town of Berwick upon Tweed, for any English plantation in America, Asia, or Africa, sufficient bond shall be given with one surety to the chief officers of the custom-house of such port or place from whence the said ship shall set sail, to the value of one thousand pounds, if the ship be of less burden than one hundred tons; and of the sum of two thousand pounds, if the ship shall be of greater burden; that in case the said ship or vessel shall load any of the said commodities at any of the said English plantations, that the same commodities shall be by the said ship brought to some port of England, Ireland, Wales, or to the port or town of Berwick upon Tweed, and shall there unload and put on shore the same, the danger of the seas only excepted; (2) and for all ships coming from any other port or place to any of the aforesaid plantations, who by this act are permitted to trade there, that the governor of such English plantations shall before the said ship or vessel be permitted to load on board any of the said commodities, take bond in manner and to the value aforesaid, for each respective ship or vessel, that such ship or vessel shall carry all the aforesaid goods that shall be laden on board in the said ship to some other of his Majesty's English plantations, or to England, Ireland, Wales, or town of Berwick upon Tweed; (3) and that every ship or vessel which shall load or take on board any of the aforesaid goods, until such bond given to the said governor, or certificate produced from the officers of any custom-house of England, Ireland, Wales, or of the town of Berwick, that such bonds have been there duly given, shall be forfeited with all her guns, tackle, apparel, and furniture, to be employed and recovered in manner as aforesaid; and the said governors and every of them shall twice in every year after the first day of January one thousand six hundred and sixty, return true copies of all such bonds by him so taken, to the chief officers of the custom in London.

The Statutes at Large, ed. D. Pickering (1762–1807), vii.452-4, 459-60

2 Attempt at Price Regulation, 1675

The fluctuations in prices of goods and services troubled colonials. From time to time laws were passed in an effort to regulate prices. The law of 3 November 1675, passed in Massachusetts, is characteristic of an effort that failed more often than it succeeded.

Whereas there is oppression in the midst of us, not only by such shop-keepers and merchants who set excessive prices on their goods, also by mechanics, but *also by mechanics* and day labourers who are daily guilty of that evil, for redress whereof and as an addition to the law, title Oppression, it is ordered by this court that any person that judgeth himself oppressed by shopkeepers or merchants in setting excessive prices on their goods, have hereby liberty to make their complaint to the grand jurors, or otherwise by petition to the county court immediately, who shall send to the person accused, and if the court, upon examination, judge the person complaining injured, they shall cause the offender to return double the overplus, or more than the equal price, to the injured person, and also impose a fine on the offenders at the discretion of the court; and if any person judge himself oppressed by mechanics or day labourers, they may make complaint thereof to the selectmen of the town, who if upon the examination do find such complaint just, having respect to the quality of the pay, and the length or shortness of the day labour, they shall cause the offender to make double restitution to the party injured, and pay a fine of double the value exceeding the due price.

Records of . . . Massachusetts Bay, ed. N. B.
Shurtleff (1853-4), v.62-3

3 Method of Obtaining Land, 1697

Land was the basis of wealth in the agrarian colonies and was eagerly sought. In the days of early settlement in Virginia, each emigrant from England was granted fifty acres of land as a 'headright' and fifty acres for each person whom he brought with him. One rascally adventurer was accused of giving Christian names to his livestock and collecting fifty acres on each cow, horse, and pig in his possession. Abuses in the granting of land were common, and great land-holders managed to obtain immense tracts. The excerpt below is taken from a report made to the Board of Trade by three Virginians.

The method settled by the king from the first seating of that country was to allot 50 acres of land to everyone that should adventure into that country; which, if it had been punctually observed, would have been a lasting encouragement to adventurers, till the country had come to be well peopled; but as the matter has been managed, the land is now gone from the king, and yet the country but very ill peopled. The first great abuse of this design was by the ignorance and knavery of surveyors, who often gave out draughts of surveys without ever actually surveying it, or ever coming on the land; only they gave the description, by some natural bounds, and were sure to allow large measure, that so the persons for whom they surveyed might enjoy larger tracts of land than they were to pay quit-rent for. Then all courts were very lavish in allowing certificates for rights; for if a master of a ship came into any court and made oath that he had imported himself and so many seamen and passengers at divers times into the country, and that he never elsewhere made use of those rights; he had presently an order granted him for so many rights (*i.e.* so many times 50 acres of land), and these rights he would sell and dispose of for a small matter. Perhaps the same seamen made oath that they had adventured themselves so many times into the country, and had not elsewhere proved their rights, and upon this they had an order for so many rights *toties quoties*. The masters likewise that bought the servants so imported would at another court make oath that they had bought so many persons that had ventured themselves into the country, and upon this so many rights were ordered them: so that still the land went away, and the adventurers themselves, who remained in the country, for whom it was originally designed, had the least share. Then great liberty was used in issuing out certificates for rights, by the country clerks, and especially by the clerks of the secretary's office, which was and is still a constant mint of these rights, where they may be purchased at very easy rates, of the clerks, from five shillings to one shilling per right.

These things were not unknown to the government, who connived at them, thinking it a very pardonable crime that the king's land was given away to people that really and truly had no right to it, since by this means the land was taken up, and so the king had so much more quit-rents paid him, whereas that which was not taken up, paid nothing. But they little considered that the small profit which comes by quit-rents doth not balance the great damage of leaving the country without inhabitants, which is the effect of the methods they have followed, for the king and kingdom of England gain near 200 times as much by an ordinary planter as the king would have got by the quit-rents of the 50 acres he should have had, which may be made out thus: an usual crop of tobacco for one head is 2,000 pounds weight, which at sixpence per pound, the present duty in England, amounts to 50 pounds. Then supposing this 2,000 pounds of tobacco to be put into 3 hogsheads, here is six shillings of Virginia duty to the king, by the 2 shillings per hogshead; then the freight of this at 8 pounds per tun comes to six pound, which is commonly paid into England; in all 56 pounds, 6 shillings; besides the increase of ships and seamen, and the multitudes maintained by the manufacture of tobacco here in England, and the manufacture of English goods sold to the planters. To find out, on the other hand, how many acres of land it will require to make up the bare 56 pounds, 6 shillings out of the quit-rents of it in quit-rent tobacco, sold *communibus annis* at 5 shillings per hundred, and 24 pounds of tobacco for every hundred acres; at that rate, 56 pounds 6 shillings, will purchase 22,520 pounds of tobacco, which is the quit-rent for 93,833 acres of land; so that one man's labour is equivalent to the quit-rents of near a hundred thousand acres of land, which was the quantity allotted for 2,000 men. Besides the quit-rents would not have been lost, but would have been paid at last when the country came to be peopled. This fundamental error of letting the king's land lie waste, together with another of not seating in townships, as they did in some other colonies, is the cause that Virginia at this day is so badly peopled.

Everyone that takes out a patent for any dividend or tract of king's land is, in the patent, obliged to two things. One is to seat or plant upon it within three years after the date of the patent, otherwise it lapses again to the king. The other is, to pay the quit-rents, at the rate of a shilling for every 50 acres *per annum*. Seating, by their law, is reckoned the building of a house, and keeping a stock one whole year. They matter not how small an house it is; if it be but a hoghouse, it serves the turn; and planting, their law reckons the planting and tending one acre of ground, it is no matter how badly, and either of these; viz. either seating or planting, within the three years, saves the whole tract, if it be never so large, which is the cause that though all the good land of the country is taken up, yet there is very little improvement on it. . . .

Henry Hartwell, James Blair, and Edward
Chilton, The Present State of Virginia, ed. H.
D. Farish (1940), pp. 16-19

4 Hat Act, 1732

Parliament passed a long series of acts designed to protect industry at home and discourage manufactures in the colonies. Typical of this type of restriction was the Hat Act, passed on 1 June 1732.

Whereas the art and mystery of making hats in Great Britain hath arrived to great perfection, and considerable quantities of hats manufactured in this kingdom have heretofore been exported to his Majesty's plantations or colonies in America, who have been wholly supplied with hats from Great Britain; and whereas great quantities of hats have of late years been made, and the said manufacture is daily increasing in the British plantations in America, and is from thence exported to foreign markets, which were heretofore supplied from Great Britain, and the hatmakers in the said plantations take many apprentices for very small terms, to the discouragement of the said trade, and debasing the said manufacture; wherefore for preventing the said ill practices for the future, and for promoting and encouraging the trade of making hats in Great Britain, be it enacted by the king's most excellent Majesty, by and with the advice and consent of the Lords Spiritual and Temporal, and Commons in this present Parliament assembled, and by the authority of the same, that from and after the twenty-ninth day of September in the year of our Lord one thousand seven hundred and thirty-two, no hats or felts whatsoever, dyed or undyed, finished or unfinished, shall be shipt, loaden, or put on board any ship or vessel in any place or parts within any of the British plantations, upon any pretence whatsoever, by any person or persons whatsoever, and also that no hats or felts, either dyed or undyed, finished or unfinished, shall be loaden upon any horse, cart, or other carriage, to the intent or purpose to be exported, transported, shipped off, carried, or conveyed out of any of the said British plantations to any other of the British plantations, or to any other place whatsoever, by any person or persons whatsoever. . . .

VII. And it is hereby further enacted by the authority aforesaid, that no person residing in any of his Majesty's plantations in America shall, from and after the said twenty-ninth day of September, one thousand seven hundred and thirty-two, make or cause to be made, any felt or hat of or with any wool or stuff whatsoever, unless he shall have first served as an apprentice in the trade or art of feltmaking during the space of seven years at the least; neither shall any feltmaker or hatmaker in any of the said plantations employ, retain, or set to work, in the said art or trade, any person as a journeyman or hired servant, other than such as shall have lawfully served an apprenticeship in the said trade for the space of seven years; nor shall any feltmaker or hatmaker in any of the said plantations have, take, or keep above the number of two apprentices at one time, or take any apprentice for any less term than seven years, upon pain to forfeit and pay the sum of five pounds for every month that he shall continue offending in the premises contrary to the true meaning of this act. . . .

Statutes at Large, xvi.304-5, 307

5 The Molasses Act, 1733

The Molasses Act was designed to benefit the British colonies in the West Indies that produced sugar and molasses. The North American colonies had found a cheaper source for the raw materials of rum in the French and Spanish islands. The Molasses Act was expected to prevent this trade with the foreign islands, but widespread smuggling made it ineffective.

Whereas the welfare and prosperity of your Majesty's sugar colonies in America are of the greatest consequence and importance to the trade, navigation, and strength of this kingdom; and whereas the planters of the said sugar colonies have of late years fallen under such great discouragements that they are unable to improve or carry on the sugar trade upon an equal footing with the foreign sugar colonies without some advantage and relief be given to them from Great Britain; for remedy whereof, . . . be it enacted . . . that from and after the twenty-fifth day of December, one thousand seven hundred and thirty-three, there shall be raised, levied, collected and paid, unto and for the use of his Majesty, his heirs and successors, upon all rum or spirits of the produce or manufacture of any of the colonies or plantations in America, not in the possession or under the dominion of his Majesty, his heirs and successors, which at any time or times within or during the continuance of this act, shall be imported or brought into any of the colonies or plantations in America, which now are or hereafter may be in the possession or under the dominion of his Majesty, his heirs or successors, the sum of nine pence, money of Great Britain, to be paid according to the proportion and value of five shillings and six pence the ounce in silver, for every gallon thereof, and after that rate for any greater or lesser quantity; and upon all molasses or syrups of such foreign produce or manufacture as aforesaid, which shall be imported or brought into any of the said colonies or plantations of or belonging to his Majesty, the sum of six pence of like money for every gallon thereof, and after that rate for any greater or lesser quantity; and upon all sugars and panelas [brown sugar] of such foreign growth, produce or manufacture as aforesaid which shall be imported into any of the said colonies or plantations of or belonging to his Majesty, a duty after the rate of five shillings of like money, for every hundredweight avoirdupois, of the said sugar and panelas, and after that rate for a greater or lesser quantity.

Statutes at Large, xvi.374

6   Rice, Corn, and Indigo with Slave Labour, c. 1749

Governor James Glen of South Carolina made a report to the Board of Trade on economic conditions in the colony in response to inquiries sent out from London in 1749. His report was surreptitiously published in London in 1761 with the title of *A Description of South Carolina*.

. . . The country [of South Carolina] abounds everywhere with large swamps, which, when cleared, opened, and sweetened by culture, yield plentiful crops of rice. Along the banks of our rivers and creeks there are also swamps and marches, fit either for rice, or, by the hardness of their bottoms, for pasturage.

It would open too large a field to enter very minutely into the nature of the soil; and I think that this will sufficiently appear by the following account of what the labour of one Negro employed on our best lands will annually produce in rice, corn, and indigo.

The best land for rice is a wet, deep, miry soil such as is generally to be found in cypress swamps; or a black, greasy mould with a clay foundation; but the very best lands may be meliorated by laying them under water at proper seasons.

Good crops are produced even the first year when the surface of the earth appears in some degree covered with the trunks and branches of trees. The proper months for sowing rice are March, April, and May.

The method is to plant it in trenches or rows made with a hoe, about three inches deep. The land must be kept pretty clear from weeds and at the latter end of August or the beginning of September it will be fit to be reaped.

Rice is not the worse for being a little green when cut. They let it remain on the stubble till dry, which will be in about two or three days, if the weather be favourable, and then they house or put it in large stacks.

Afterwards it is threshed with a flail, and then winnowed, which was formerly a very tedious operation, but it is now performed with great ease by a very simple machine, a wind-fan, but lately used here and a prodigious improvement.

The next part of the process is grinding, which is done in small mills made of wood of about two feet in diameter. It is then winnowed again, and afterwards put into a mortar made of wood, sufficient to contain from half a bushel to a bushel, where it is beat with a pestle of a size suitable to the mortar and to the strength of the person who is to pound it. This is done to free the rice from a thick skin, and is the most laborious part of the work.

It is then sifted from the flour and dust, made by the pounding, and afterwards by a wire sieve called a market sieve it is separated from the broken and small rice, which fits it for the barrels in which it is carried to market.

They reckon thirty slaves a proper number for a rice plantation, and to be tended with one overseer. . . .

Indian corn delights in high loose land. It does not agree with clay, and is killed by much wet. It is generally planted in ridges made by the plough or hoe, and in holes about six or eight feet from each other. It requires to be kept free from weeds, and will produce, according to the goodness of the land, from fifteen to fifty bushels an acre; some extraordinary rich land in good seasons will yield eighty bushels, but the common computation is that a Negro will tend six acres and that each acre will produce from ten to thirty-five bushels. It sells generally for about ten shillings currency a bushel, but is at present fifteen.

Indigo is of several sorts. What we have gone mostly upon is the sort generally cultivated in the Sugar Islands, which requires a high loose soil, tolerably rich, and is an annual plant; but the wild sort, which is common in this country, is much more hardy and luxuriant, and is perennial. Its stalk dies every year, but it shoots up again next spring. The indigo made from it is of as good a quality as the other, and it will grow on very indifferent land, provided it be dry and loose.

An acre of good land may produce about eighty pounds weight of good indigo, and one slave may manage two acres and upwards, and raise provisions besides, and have all the winter months to saw lumber and be otherwise employed in. But as much of the land hitherto used for indigo is improper, I am persuaded that not above thirty pounds weight of good indigo per acre can be expected from the land at present cultivated. Perhaps we are not conversant enough in this commodity, either in the culture of the plant or in the method of managing or manufacturing it, to write with certainty. . . .

But I cannot leave this subject without observing how conveniently and profitably, as to the charge of labour, both indigo and rice may be managed by the same persons; for the labour attending indigo being over in the summer months, those who were employed in it may afterwards manufacture rice in the ensuing part of the year, when it becomes most laborious; and after doing all this they will have some time to spare for sawing lumber, and making hogshead and other staves to supply the Sugar Colonies.

> Reprinted in *Colonial South Carolina*, ed.
> Chapman J. Milling (1951), pp. 6–10

7   The Iron Act, 1750

The mercantilist theory permitted the manufacture of certain crude products in the colonies that could be reworked or refined in England. The Iron Act illustrates this type of legislation, which encouraged the production of pig-iron in the colonies but made the manufacture of steel and finished iron products illegal.

Whereas the importation of bar iron from his Majesty's colonies in America, into the port of London, and the importation of pig-iron from the said colonies into any port of Great Britain, and the manufacture of such bar and pig-iron in Great Britain, will be a great advantage not only to the said colonies, but also to this kingdom, by furnishing the manufacturers of iron with a supply of that useful and necessary commodity; and by means thereof large sums of money, now annually paid for iron to foreigners, will be saved to this kingdom, and a greater quantity of the woollen, and other manufactures of Great Britain, will be exported to America in exchange for such iron so imported; be it therefore enacted by the king's most excellent Majesty, by and with the advice and consent of the Lords Spiritual and Temporal, and Commons, in this present Parliament assembled, and by the authority of the same, that from and after the twenty-fourth day of June, one thousand seven hundred and fifty, the several and respective subsidies, customs, impositions, rates, and duties, now payable on pig-iron, made in and imported from his Majesty's colonies in America, into any port of Great Britain, shall cease, determine, and be no longer paid: and that from and after the said twenty-fourth day of June, no subsidy, custom, imposition, rate or duty whatsoever shall be payable upon bar-iron made in and imported from the said colonies into the port of London; any law statute, or usage to the contrary thereof in any wise notwithstanding.

IX. And, that pig and bar-iron made in his Majesty's colonies in America may be further manufactured in this kingdom, be it further enacted by the authority aforesaid, that from and after the twenty-fourth day of June, one thousand seven hundred and fifty, no mill or other engine for slitting or rolling of iron, or any plating-forge to work with a tilt hammer, or any furnace for making steel, shall be erected, or after such erection, continued, in any of his Majesty's colonies in America; and if any person or persons shall erect, or cause to be erected, or after such erection, continue, or cause to be continued, in any of the said colonies, any such mill, engine, forge, or furnace, every person or persons so offending, shall for every such mill, engine, forge, or furnace, forfeit the sum of two hundred pounds of lawful money of Great Britain.

Statutes at Large, xx.97, 99-100

8 Slaves Forced upon Colonies, 1757

The Royal African Company, which held a virtual monopoly of the slave trade to the English colonies, industriously pushed the sale of Africans. A Virginia preacher, Peter Fontaine, in reply to a query, explained the workings of the slave trade.

As to your second query, if enslaving our fellow creatures be a practice agreeable to Christianity, it is answered in a great measure in many treatises at home, to which I refer you. I shall only mention something of our present state here.

Like Adam we are all apt to shift off the blame from ourselves and lay it upon others, how justly in our case you may judge. The Negroes are enslaved by the Negroes themselves before they are purchased by the masters of the ships who bring them here. It is to be sure at our choice whether we buy them or not, so this then is our crime, folly, or whatever you will please to call it. But, our Assembly, foreseeing the ill consequences of importing such numbers amongst us, hath often attempted to lay a duty upon them which would amount to a prohibition, such as ten or twenty pounds a head, but no governor dare pass such a law, having instructions to the contrary from the Board of Trade at home. By this means they are forced upon us whether we will or will not. This plainly shows the African Company hath the advantage of the colonies, and may do as it pleases with the ministry.

Indeed, since we have been exhausted of our little stock of cash by the war, the importation has stopped; our poverty then is our best security. There is no more picking for their ravenous jaws upon bare bones, but should we begin to thrive, they will be at the same again. All our taxes are now laid upon slaves and on shippers of tobacco, which they wink at while we are in danger of being torn from them, but we durst not do it in time of peace, it being looked upon as the highest presumption to lay any burden upon trade. This is our part of the grievance, but to live in Virginia without slaves is morally impossible. Before our troubles, you could not hire a servant or slave for love or money, so that unless robust enough to cut wood, to go to mill, to work at the hoe, etc., you must starve, or board in some family where they both fleece and half starve you. There is no set price upon corn, wheat and provisions, so they take advantage of the necessities of strangers, who are thus obliged to purchase some slaves and land. This of course draws us all into the original sin and curse of the country of purchasing slaves, and this is the reason we have no merchants, traders, or artificers of any sort but what become planters in a short time.

A common labourer, white or black, if you can be so much favoured as to hire one, is a shilling sterling or fifteen pence currency per day; a bungling carpenter two shillings or two shillings and sixpence per day; besides diet and lodging. That is, for a lazy fellow to get wood and water, £19. 16. 3, current per annum; add to this seven or eight pounds more and you have a slave for life.

> Peter Fontaine, letter to his brother Moses (1757), printed in *Memoirs of a Huguenot Family*, ed. A. Maury (1853), pp. 351-2

9 Currency in the Colonies, 1704

The problem of sufficient currency to carry on business continually vexed the colonies. Imposts and duties had to be paid in specie and the quantity in circulation was always insufficient to meet normal needs. Consequently foreign coins, some obtained in illegal trade, circulated freely. The royal proclamation of 1704 attempted to stabilize the value of foreign coins and to give them the same value in all colonies.

We having had under our consideration the different rates at which the same species of foreign coins do pass in our several colonies and plantations in America, and the inconveniences thereof, by the indirect practice of drawing the money from one plantation to another to the great prejudice of the trade of our subjects; and being sensible that the same cannot be otherwise remedied than by reducing of all foreign coins to the same current rate within all our dominions in America; and the principal officers of our mint having laid before us a table of the value of the several foreign coins which usually pass in payments in our said plantations, according to their weight and the assays made of them in our mint, thereby showing the just proportion which each coin ought to have to the other, which is as followeth, viz.: Seville pieces of eight, old plate, seventeen pennyweight twelve grains, four shillings and six pence; Seville pieces of eight, new plate, fourteen penny-weight three shillings seven pence one farthing; Mexico pieces of eight, seventeen pennyweight twelve grains, four shillings and six pence; Pillar pieces of eight, seventeen pennyweight twelve grains, four shillings and six pence three farthings; Peru pieces of eight, old plate, seventeen pennyweight twelve grains, four shillings and five pence, or thereabouts; cross dollars, eighteen pennyweight, four shillings and four pence three farthings; ducatoons of Flanders, twenty pennyweight and twenty-one grains, five shillings and six pence; ecus of France, or silver louis, seventeen pennyweight twelve grains, four shillings and six pence; crusadoes of Portugal, eleven pennyweight four grains, two shillings and ten pence one farthing; three guilder pieces of Holland, twenty pennyweight and seven grains, five shillings and two pence one farthing; old rix-dollars of the Empire, eighteen pennyweight and ten grains, four shillings and six pence; the half, quarters and other parts in proportion to their denominations, and light pieces in proportion to their weight. We have therefore thought fit for remedying the said inconveniences, by the advice of our Council, to publish and declare, that from and after the first day of January next ensuing the date hereof, no Seville, Pillar, or Mexico pieces of eight, though of the full weight of seventeen pennyweight and a half, shall be accounted, received, taken or paid within any of our said colonies or plantations, as well those under proprietors and charters, as under our immediate commission and government, at above the rate of six shillings per piece current money, for the discharge of any contracts or bargains to be made after the said first day of January next, the halfs, quarters, and other lesser pieces of the same coins to be accounted, received, taken, or paid in the same proportion. And the currency of all pieces of eight of Peru, dollars, and other foreign species of silver coins, whether of the same or baser alloy, shall, after the said first day of January next, stand regulated, according to their weight and fineness, according and in proportion to the rate before limited and set for the pieces of eight of Seville, Pillar, and Mexico; so that no foreign silver coin of any sort be permitted to exceed the same proportion upon any account whatsoever. And we do hereby require and command all our governors, lieutenant-governors, magistrates, officers, and all other our good subjects, within our said colonies and plantations, to observe and obey our directions herein, as they tender our displeasure.

Given at our castle at Windsor, the eighteenth day of June 1704 in the third year of our reign.

British Royal Proclamations Relating to America, 1603-1783 (American Antiquarian Society *Transactions*, xii, 1911), pp. 161-3

VI

RELATIONS WITH THE INDIANS

1 Thomas Hariot Reports on American Indians, 1588

Although Raleigh's Roanoke colony disappeared with scarcely a trace, it contributed valuable information for future colonists. The most important account of early English relations with American Indians is included in a description of the colony by Thomas Hariot, a scientist sent by Raleigh with the 1585 expedition. Written to gain further support for the enterprise, Hariot's tract reports the best features of the new land and its inhabitants.

OF THE NATURE AND MANNERS OF THE PEOPLE

It resteth I speak a word or two of the natural inhabitants, their natures and manners, leaving large discourse thereof until time more convenient hereafter. Now only so far forth as that you may know how that they, in respect of troubling our inhabiting and planting, are not to be feared; but that they shall have cause both to fear and love us, that shall inhabit with them.

They are a people clothed with loose mantles made of deerskins & aprons of the same round about their middles; all else naked; of such a difference of statures only as we in England. Having no edge tools or weapons of iron or steel to offend us withal, neither know they how to make any. Those weapons that they have are only bows made of witch hazel & arrows of reeds; flat-edged truncheons, also of wood, about a yard long. Neither have they anything to defend themselves but targets made of barks and some armours made of sticks wickered together with thread.

Their towns are but small, & near the sea-coast but few, some containing but 10 or 12 houses, some 20. The greatest that we have seen have been but of 30 houses. If they be walled, it is only done with barks of trees made fast to stakes, or else with poles only fixed upright and close one by another.

Their houses are made of small poles made fast at the tops in round form after the manner as is used in many arbories in our gardens of England; in most towns covered with barks, and in some with artificial mats made of long rushes, from the tops of the houses down to the ground. The length of them is commonly double to the breadth. In some places they are but 12 and 16 yards long, and in other some we have seen of four and twenty.

In some places of the country one only town belongeth to the government of a werowance, or chief lord; in other some two or three, in some six, eight, & more. The greatest werowance that yet we had dealing with had but eighteen towns in his government, and able to make not above seven or eight hundred fighting men at the most. The language of every government is different from any other, and the farther they are distant the greater is the difference.

Their manner of wars amongst themselves is either by sudden surprising one another, most commonly about the dawning of the day or moonlight, or else by ambushes or some subtle devices. Set battles are very rare, except it fall out where there are many trees, where either part may have some hope of defence after the delivery of every arrow, in leaping behind some or other.

If there fall out any wars between us & them, what their fight is likely to be – we having advantages against them so many manner of ways, as by our discipline, our strange weapons and devices else, especially by ordnance great and small – it may be easily imagined. By the experience we have had in some places, the turning up of their heels against us in running away was their best defence.

In respect of us they are a people poor, and, for want of skill and judgement in the knowledge and use of our things, do esteem our trifles before things of greater value. Notwithstanding, in their proper manner, considering the want of such means as we have, they seem very ingenious. For although they have no such tools, nor any such crafts, sciences, and arts as we, yet in those things they do, they show excellency of wit. And by how much they, upon due consideration, shall find our manner of knowledges and crafts to exceed theirs in perfection and speed for doing or execution, by so much the more is it probable that they should desire our friendships & love, and have the greater respect for pleasing and obeying us. Whereby may be hoped, if means of good government be used, that they may in short time be brought to civility and the embracing of true religion.

Some religion they have already which, although it be far from the truth, yet, being as it is, there is hope it may be the easier and sooner reformed.

They believe that there are many gods, which they call Mantóac, but of different sorts and degrees; one only chief and great God, which hath been from all eternity. Who, as they affirm, when he purposed to make the world, made first other gods of a principal order to be as means and instruments to be used in the creation and government to follow; and after, the sun, moon, and stars as petty gods and the instruments of the other order more principal. First, they say, were made waters, out of which by the gods was made all diversity of creatures that are visible or invisible.

For mankind, they say a woman was made first which, by the working of one of the gods, conceived and brought forth children. And in such sort they say they had their beginning.

But how many years or ages have passed since, they say they can make no relation, having no letters nor other such means as we to keep records of the particularities of times past, but only tradition from father to son. . . .

They believe also the immortality of the soul, that after this life, as soon as the soul is departed from the body, according to the works it hath done it is either carried to heaven, the habitacle of gods, there to enjoy perpetual bliss and happiness, or else to a great pit or hole, which they think to be in the furthest parts of their part of the world toward the sunset, there to burn continually. The place they call *Popogusso*. . . .

What subtlety soever be in the werowances and priests, this opinion worketh so much in many of the common and simple sort of people that it maketh them have great respect to their governors, and also great care what they do, to avoid torment after death and to enjoy bliss. Although, notwithstanding, there is punishment ordained for malefactors – as stealers, whoremongers, and other sorts of wicked doers; some punished with death, some with forfeitures, some with beating, according to the greatness of the facts. . . .

Most things they saw with us, as mathematical instruments, sea compasses, the virtue of the loadstone in drawing iron, a perspective glass whereby was showed many strange sights, burning glasses, wildfire works, guns, books, writing and reading, spring clocks that seem to go of themselves, and many other things that we had, were so strange unto them, and so far exceeded their capacities to comprehend the reason and means how they should be made and done, that they thought they were rather the works of gods than of men, or, at the leastwise, they had been given and taught us of the gods. Which made many of them to have such opinion of us as that, if they knew not the truth of God and religion already, it was rather to be had from us, whom God so specially loved, than from a people that were so simple, as they found themselves to be in comparison of us. . . .

There could at no time happen any strange sickness, losses, hurts, or any other cross unto them but that they would impute to us the cause or means thereof for offending or not pleasing us.

One other rare and strange accident . . . which moved the whole country that either knew or heard of us to have us in wonderful admiration: There was no town where we had any subtle device practised against us (we leaving it unpunished or not revenged because we sought by all means possible to win them by gentleness) but that, within a few days after our departure from every such town, the people began to die very fast, and many in short space; in some towns about twenty, in some forty, in some sixty, & in one six score, which, in truth, was very many in respect of their numbers. This happened in no place that we could learn but where we had been, where they used some practice against us, and after such time. The disease also so strange that they neither knew what it was nor how to cure it. The like, by report of the oldest men in the country, never happened before, time out of mind. A thing specially observed by us as also by the natural inhabitants themselves.

Insomuch that when some of the inhabitants which were our friends, & especially the werowance *Wingina*, had observed such effects in four or five towns to follow their wicked practices, they were persuaded that it was the work of our God through our means, and that we, by Him, might kill and slay whom we would without weapons and not come near them. . . .

This marvelous accident in all the country wrought so strange opinions of us that some people could not tell whether to think us gods or men;

and the rather because that, all the space of their sickness, there was no man of ours known to die, or that was specially sick. They noted also that we had no women amongst us, neither that we did care for any of theirs.

Some, therefore, were of opinion that we were not born of women, and therefore not mortal, but that we were men of an old generation many years past then risen again to immortality. . . . Those that were immediately to come after us they imagined to be in the air, yet invisible & without bodies, & that they, by our entreaty & for the love of us, did make the people to die in that sort as they did by shooting invisible bullets into them. . . .

These their opinions I have set down the more at large that it may appear unto you that there is good hope they may be brought, through discreet dealing and government, to the embracing of the truth and, consequently, to honour, obey, fear, and love us.

And although some of our company towards the end of the year showed themselves too fierce, in slaying some of the people, in some towns, upon causes that on our part might easily enough have been born withal, yet notwithstanding, because it was on their part justly deserved, the alteration of their opinions generally & for the most part concerning us is the less to be doubted. And whatsoever else they may be, by carefulness of ourselves, need nothing at all to be feared.

> Thomas Hariot, *A Brief and True Report of the New Found Land of Virginia* (1588), reprinted in Hakluyt, *Principal Navigations* (1589) and in Theodor de Bry, *America*, pt. 1 (1590). A collation of above texts printed in *The Roanoke Voyages*, ed. D. B. Quinn (Hakluyt Society, 1955), i.368–82

2   Virginia Massacre, 1622

Not surprisingly, the colonists did not maintain their god-like image in the eyes of natives who watched a steady encroachment by the white men upon their lands. In a sudden uprising in 1622, the Indians attempted to rid themselves of the Virginia colony. A contemporary report of the massacre by the secretary of the Virginia Company (*a*) omitted the immediate cause of the uprising, stated in Captain John Smith, *General History of Virgina* (*b*). The Council for Virginia in London was more critical than sympathetic (*c*). Some were victims of both sides (*d*).

(*a*) A RELATION OF THE BARBAROUS MASSACRE IN THE TIME OF PEACE AND LEAGUE, TREACHEROUSLY EXECUTED BY THE NATIVE INFIDELS UPON THE ENGLISH, the 22 of March Last

... By this [preliminary description of Virginia] ... the reader may understand the great riches and blessings of this excellent country, which even ordinary diligence and care must needs strangely improve.

But that all men may see the unpartial ingenuity of this discourse, we freely confess that the country is not so good as the natives are bad, whose barbarous savageness needs more cultivation than the ground itself, being more overspread with incivility than that with briers. ... The last May there came letters from Sir Francis Wyatt, Governor in Virginia, which did advertise that when in November last he arrived in Virginia and entered upon his government he found the country settled in a peace (as all men there thought) sure and unviolable, not only because it was solemnly ratified and sworn and, at the request of the native king, stamped in brass and fixed to one of his oaks of note, but as being advantageous to both parts: to the savages as the weaker, under which they were safely sheltered and defended; to us as being the easiest way then thought to pursue and advance our projects of buildings, plantings, and effecting their conversion by peaceable and fair means. And such was the conceit of firm peace and amity as that there was seldom or never a sword worn, and a piece seldomer, except for a deer or fowl. By which assurance of security the plantations of particular adventurers and planters were placed scatteringly and stragglingly as a choice vein of rich ground invited them, and the further from neighbours held the better; the houses generally set open to the savages, who were always friendly entertained at the tables of the English and commonly lodged in their bedchambers. ...

And as well on the Friday morning (the fatal day), the twenty-second of March, as also in the evening, as in other days before, they came unarmed into our houses, without bows or arrows or other weapons, with deer, turkeys, fish, furs, and other provisions, to sell and truck with us for glass, beads, and other trifles, Yea, in some places sat down at breakfast with our people at their tables, whom immediately, with their own tools and weapons, either laid down or standing in their houses, they basely and barbarously murdered, not sparing either age or sex, man, woman, or child; so sudden in their cruel execution, that few or none discerned the weapon or blow that brought them to destruction. In which manner they also slew many of our people then at their several works and husbandries in the fields and without their houses, some in planting corn and tobacco, some in gardening, some in making brick, building, sawing, and other kinds of husbandry.... And by this means that fatal Friday morning there fell under the bloody and barbarous hands of that perfidious and inhuman people, contrary to all laws of God and men, of nature and nations, 347 men, women, and children, most by their own weapons. And not being content with taking away life alone, they fell after again upon the dead, making as well as they could a fresh murder, defacing, dragging, and mangling the dead carcasses into many pieces and carrying some parts away in derision with base and brutish triumph....

That worthy religious gentleman, Master George Thorpe, Esquire, deputy of the College lands, sometimes one of His Majesty's pensioners, and in one of the principal places of command in Virginia, did so truly and earnestly affect their conversion and was so tender over them that whosoever under his authority had given them but the least displeasure or discontent he punished them severely. He thought nothing too dear for them, and, as being desirous to bind them unto him by his many courtesies, he never denied them anything that they asked him. ... He was not only too kind and beneficial to the common sort but also to their king, to whom he oft resorted and gave many presents which he knew to be highly pleasing to him. And whereas this king before dwelt only in a cottage, or rather a den or hogsty, made with a few poles and sticks and covered with mats after their wild manner, to civilize him he first built him a fair house according to the English fashion, in which he took such joy, especially in his lock and key, which he so admired as, locking and unlocking his door an hundred times a day, he thought no device in all the world was comparable to it. ... And both he and his people, for the daily courtesies this good gentleman did to one or other of them, did profess such outward love and respect unto him as nothing could seem more. But all was little regarded after by this viperous brood, as the sequel showed: for they not only wilfully murdered him but cruelly and felly, out of devilish malice, did so many barbarous despites and foul scorns after to his dead corpse as are unbefitting to be heard by any civil ear. ...

Yet it pleased God to use some of them as instruments to save many of their lives whose souls they had formerly saved, as at James City and other places . . . all whose lives were saved by a converted Indian disclosing the plot in the instant. . . . Such was (God be thanked for it) the good fruit of an infidel converted to Christianity; for though three hundred and more of ours died by many of these pagan infidels, yet thousands of ours were saved by the means of one of them alone which was made a Christian. . . .

That the true cause of this surprise was most by the instigation of the devil (enemy to their salvation); and the daily fear that possessed them that in time we, by our growing continually upon them, would dispossess them of this country, as they had been formerly of the West Indies by the Spaniard, produced this bloody act. That never grief and shame possessed any people more than themselves to be thus butchered by so naked and cowardly a people, who dare not stand the presentment of a staff in manner of a piece, nor an uncharged piece in the hands of a woman, from which they fly as so many hares much faster than from their tormenting devil, whom they worship for fear, though they acknowledge they love him not. . . .

Edward Waterhouse, A Declaration of the State
of the Colony . . . in Virginia (1622)

(b) THE MASSACRE UPON THE TWO AND TWENTIETH OF MARCH

The prologue to this tragedy is supposed was occasioned by Nemattanow, otherwise called Jack of the Feather because he commonly was most strangely adorned with them, and for his courage and policy was accounted amongst the savages their chief captain and immortal from any hurt could be done him by the English. This captain, coming to one Morgan's house, knowing he had many commodities that he desired, persuaded Morgan to go with him to Pamunkey to truck, but the savage murdered him by the way. And after two or three days returned again to Morgan's house, where he found two youths, his servants, who asked for their master. Jack replied directly he was dead; the boys, suspecting as it was by seeing him wear his cap, would have had him to Master Thorpe, but Jack so moved their patience they shot him so he fell to the ground, put him in a boat to have him before the Governor, then seven or eight miles from them. But by the way Jack, finding the pangs of death upon him, desired of the boys two things: the one was that they would not make it known he was slain with a bullet, the other to bury him amongst the English.

At the loss of this savage Opechancanough much grieved and repined, with great threats of revenge; but the English returned him such terrible answers that he cunningly dissembled his intent with the greatest signs he could of love and peace; yet within fourteen days after he acted what followeth. . . .

Smith, *General History* (1624), Book IV, reprinted in *Narratives . . . Virginia*, ed. Tyler pp. 357ff.

(c) TREASURER AND COUNCIL FOR VIRGINIA [in London]. LETTER TO THE GOVERNOR AND COUNCIL IN VIRGINIA

To our very loving friends, Sir Francis Wyatt, Knight, Governor, and Captain General of Virginia; and to the rest of the Council of State there

August the first, 1622

After our very hearty commendations:

We have, to our extreme grief, understood of the great massacre executed on our people in Virginia, and that in such a manner as is more miserable than the death itself: to fall by the hands of men so contemptible, to be surprised by treachery in a time of known danger, to be deaf to so plain a warning as (we now too late understand) was last year given, to be secure in an occasion of so great suspicion and jealousy as was Nemattanow's death, not to perceive anything in so open and general conspiracy, but to be made in part instruments of contriving it and almost guilty of the destruction by a blindfold and stupid entertaining of it, which the least wisdom or courage sufficed to prevent even on the point of execution, are circumstances that do add much to our sorrow and make us to confess that it is the heavy hand of Almighty God for the punishment of ours and your transgression. To the humble acknowledgment and perfect amendment whereof, together with ourselves, we seriously advise and invite you, and in particular earnestly require the speedy redress of those two enormous excesses of apparel and drinking, the cry whereof cannot but have gone up to Heaven, since the infamy hath spread itself to all that have heard the name of Virginia, to the detestation of all good minds, the scorn of others, and our extreme grief and shame. In the strength of those faults, undoubtedly, and the neglect of the divine worship, have the Indians prevailed, more than in your weakness. Whence the evil therefore sprung, the remedy must first begin and an humble reconciliation be made with the Divine Majesty by future conformity unto His most just and holy laws; which doing, we doubt not but that you shall be safe from the hands of all your enemies and them that hate you, from whom, if God's protection be not with you, no strength of situation can save you, and with it we conceive not but where you be you make yourselves as secure as in any other place whatsoever: and in all other respects the change cannot be but to the worst, nay, to the utter overthrow, not only of all our labours and charges past, but to the frustrating of our intentions and hopes and the expectation of His Majesty and the whole state. . . .

These are part of the remedies that are to be applied for the repairing of this late disaster. As for the actors thereof, we cannot but with much grief proceed to the condemnation of their bodies, the saving of whose souls we have so zealously affected. But since the innocent blood of so many Christians doth in justice cry out for revenge, and your future security in wisdom require, we must advise you to root out from being any longer a people, so cursed a nation, ungrateful to all benefit and uncapable of all goodness; at least to the removal of them so far from you as you may not only be out of danger, but out of fear of them of whose faith and good meaning you can never be secure. Wherefore, as they have merited let them have a perpetual war without peace or truce; and although they have deserved it without mercy too, yet remembering who we are, rather than what they have been, we cannot but advise not only the sparing but the preservation of the younger people of both sexes, whose bodies may, by labour and service, become profitable, and their mind[s], not overgrown with evil customs, be reduced to civility and afterward to Christianity. . . .

Records of the Virginia Company of London, ed.
S. M. Kingsbury (1905-35), iii.666-7, 671-2

(d) PETITION OF JANE DICKENSON, March 30, 1624

The humble petition of Jane Dickenson, widow, most humbly showeth that whereas her late husband, Ralph Dickenson, came over into this country four years since, obliged to Nicholas Hide, deceased, for the term of seven years, he only to have for himself and your petitioner the one half of his labours, her said husband being slain in the bloody massacre and herself carried away with the cruel savages, amongst them enduring much misery for ten months, at the expiration it pleased God so to dispose the hearts of the Indians that for a small ransom your petitioner with divers others should be released. In consideration that Doctor Potts laid out two pound of beads for her releasement, he allegeth your petitioner is linked to his servitude with a twofold chain, the one for her late husband's obligation and th'other for her ransom, of both which she hopeth that in conscience she ought to be discharged: of the first by her widowhood, of the second by the law of nations, considering she hath already served ten months, too much for two pound of beads.

The premises notwithstanding, Dr. Pott[s] refuseth to set your petitioner at liberty, threatening to make him serve her [sic] the uttermost day, unless she procure him 150 pound weight of tobacco. She therefore most humbly desireth that you will be pleased to take what course shall be thought just for her releasement fro' his servitude, considering that it much differeth not from her slavery with the Indians. . . .

Records of Virginia Co., iv.473

3   Indian Relations at Plymouth, 1621-1622

Relations with the Indians at Plymouth plantation followed much the same pattern as those in Virginia: initial friendliness turning gradually to mutual distrust. The New Englanders seem to have been somewhat more sophisticated in their diplomacy, but they had the advantage of occasional news from the longer-established colony to the south.

(a) IN RESPECT OF THE INDIANS

Many years since at Plymouth plantation, when the Church did fast and pray for rain in extreme drought; it being a very hot and clear sunshine day, all the former part thereof; an Indian of good quality, being present and seeing what they were about, fell a-wondering at them for praying for rain in a day so unlikely, when all sun and no clouds appeared; and thought that their God was not able to give rain at such a time as that. But this poor wretch, seeing them still to continue in their prayers and beholding that at last the clouds began to rise, and by that time they had ended their duty the rain fell in a most sweet, constant, soaking shower, fell into wonderment at the power that the English had with their God, and the greatness and goodness of that

God whom they served. And was smitten with terror that he had abused them and their God by his former hard thoughts of them, and resolved from that day not to rest till he did know this great good God; and for that end to forsake the Indians and cleave to the English; which he presently did, and laboured by all public and private means to suck in more and more of the knowledge of God and His ways. And as he increased in knowledge, so in affection, and also in his practice, reforming and conforming himself accordingly. And though he was much tempted by enticements, scoffs, and scorns from the Indians, yet could he never be gotten from the English, nor from seeking after their God, but died amongst them, leaving some good hopes in their hearts that his soul went to rest.

2. Sagamore John, Prince of Massachusetts, was from our very first landing more courteous, ingenious, and to the English more loving than others of them. He desired to learn and speak our language, and loved to imitate us in our behaviour and apparel; and began to hearken after our God and His ways, and would much commend Englishmen and their God, saying, 'Much good men, much good God'. And, being convinced that our condition and ways were better far than theirs, did resolve and promise to leave the Indians and come live with us. But yet, kept down by fear of the scoffs of the Indians, had not power to make good his purpose. Yet went on, not without some trouble of mind and secret plucks of conscience, as the sequel declares: for, being struck with death, fearfully cried out of himself that he had not come to live with us, to have known our God better. 'But now,' said he, 'I must die. The God of the English is much angry with me and will destroy me. Ah, I was afraid of the scoffs of these wicked Indians. Yet my child shall live with the English and learn to know their God when I am dead. I'll give him to Mr. Wilson, he is much good man and much loved me.' So sent for Mr. Wilson to come to him, and committed his only child to his care, and so died.

3. Divers of the Indian children, boys and girls, we have received into our houses, who are long since civilized, and in subjection to us, painful and handy in their business, and can speak our language familiarly; divers of whom can read English, and begin to understand, in their measure, the grounds of Christian religion. Some of them are able to give us account of the sermons they hear, and of the word read and expounded in our families; and are convinced of their sinful and miserable estates, and affected with the sense of God's displeasure and the thoughts of Eternity, and will sometimes tremble and melt into

tears at our opening and pressing the Word upon their consciences. And as far as we can discern, some of them use to pray in secret, and are much in love with us, and cannot endure to return any more to the Indians. . . .

[John Eliot], *New Englands First Fruits* (1643), reprinted in S. E. Morison, *The Founding of Harvard College* (1935), Appendix D, pp. 422–3

(b) [DIPLOMATIC RELATIONS, 1621]

All this while the Indians came skulking about them, and would sometimes show themselves aloof off, but when any approached near them, they would run away; and once they stole away their tools where they had been at work and were gone to dinner. But about the 16th of March, a certain Indian came boldly amongst them and spoke to them in broken English, which they could well understand but marveled at it. At length they understood by discourse with him, that he was not of these parts, but belonged to the eastern parts where some English ships came to fish, with whom he was acquainted and could name sundry of them by their names, amongst whom he had got his language. He became profitable to them in acquainting them with many things concerning the state of the country in the east parts where he lived, which was afterwards profitable unto them; as also of the people here, of their names, number and strength, of their situation and distance from this place, and who was chief amongst them. His name was Samoset. He told them also of another Indian whose name was Squanto, a native of this place, who had been in England and could speak better English than himself.

Being, after some time of entertainment and gifts, dismissed, a while after he came again, and five more with him, and they brought again all the tools that were stolen away before, and made way for the coming of their great Sachem, called Massasoit. Who, about four or five days after, came with the chief of his friends and other attendance, with the aforesaid Squanto. With whom, after friendly entertainment and some gifts given him, they made a peace with him (which hath now continued this 24 years) in these terms:

1. That neither he nor any of his should injure or do hurt to any of their people.

2. That if any of his did hurt to any of theirs, he should send the offender, that they might punish him.

3. That if anything were taken away from any of theirs, he should cause it to be restored; and they should do the like to his.

4. If any did unjustly war against him, they would aid him; if any did war against them, he should aid them.

5. He should send to his neighbours confederates to certify them of this, that they might not wrong them, but might be likewise comprised in the conditions of peace.

6. That when their men came to them, they should leave their bows and arrows behind them.

After these things he returned to his place called Sowams, some 40 miles from this place, but Squanto continued with them and was their interpreter and was a special instrument sent of God for their good beyond their expectation. He directed them how to set their corn, where to take fish, and to procure other commodities, and was also their pilot to bring them to unknown places for their profit, and never left them till he died. He was a native of this place, and scarce any left alive besides himself. He was carried away with divers others by one Hunt, a master of a ship, who thought to sell them for slaves in Spain. But he got away for England and was entertained by a merchant in London, and employed to Newfoundland and other parts, and lastly brought hither into these parts by one Mr. Dermer, a gentleman employed by Sir Ferdinando Gorges and others for discovery and other designs in these parts. . . .

But by the former passages, and other things of like nature, they began to see that Squanto sought his own ends and played his own game, by putting the Indians in fear and drawing gifts from them to enrich himself, making them believe he could stir up war against whom he would, and make peace for whom he would. Yea, he made them believe they kept the plague buried in the ground, and could send it amongst whom they would, which did much terrify the Indians and made them depend more on him, and seek more to him, than to Massasoit. Which procured him envy and had like to have cost him his life; for after the discovery of his practices, Massasoit sought it both privately and openly which caused him to stick close to the English, and never durst go from them till he died. They also made good use of the emulation that grew between Hobomok and him, which made them carry more squarely. And the Governor seemed to countenance the one, and the Captain the other, by which they had better intelligence, and made them both more diligent. . . .

[NEWS FROM VIRGINIA, 1622]

This summer they built a fort with good timber, both strong and comely which was of good defense, made with a flat roof and battlements, on which their ordnance were mounted, and where they kept constant watch, especially in time of danger. It served them also for a meeting house and was fitted accordingly for that use. It was a great work for them in this weakness and time of wants, but the danger of the time required it; and both the continual rumors of the fears from the Indians here, especially the Narragansetts, and also the hearing of that great massacre in Virginia, made all hands willing to dispatch the same.

William Bradford, *Of Plymouth Plantation* (1606-1646), MS in Mass. State Library, Boston; first printed 1856. Most authoritative modern reprint: *Of Plymouth Plantation, 1620-1647*, ed. S. E. Morison (1952), pp. 79-81, 87-9, 96-7, 99, 111

4   The Captivity of Mary Rowlandson, 1676

Mary Rowlandson was the wife of the minister of Lancaster, Massachusetts, a frontier town of some fifty families organized for defence into six garrisons. In January 1676 warning was received from a Christian Indian that the town would probably soon be attacked. The Reverend Mr. Rowlandson and his wife's brother-in-law, Lt. Kerley, went to the Governor in Boston to appeal for help. A relief party of forty men was finally dispatched the night of 9-10 February, too late to save the Rowlandson garrison. The other five, however, held out until news of the relief caused the Indians to retire.

On the tenth of February, 1675 [1676 N.S.], came the Indians with great numbers upon Lancaster. Their first coming was about sunrising. Hearing the noise of some guns, we looked out; several houses were burning and the smoke ascending to heaven. There were five persons taken in one house: the father and the mother and a sucking child they knocked on the head; the other two they took, and carried away alive. There were two others who, being out of their garrison upon some occasion, were set upon; one was knocked on the head, the other escaped. Another there was who, running along, was shot and wounded, and fell down; he begged of them his life, promising them money (as they told me); but they would not hearken to him, but knocked

him in head, and stripped him naked, and split open his bowels. Another, seeing many of the Indians about his barn, ventured and went
out, but was quickly shot down. . . . The Indians, getting up upon the
roof of the barn, had advantage to shoot down upon them over their
fortification. Thus these murderous wretches went on, burning and
destroying before them.

At length they came and beset our own house, and quickly it was the
dolefullest day that ever mine eyes saw. The house stood upon the
edge of a hill. Some of the Indians got behind the hill, others into the
barn, and others behind anything that could shelter them; from all
which places they shot against the house, so that the bullets seemed to
fly like hail; and quickly they wounded one man among us, then
another, and then a third. About two hours (according to my observa-
tion in that amazing time) they had been about the house before they
prevailed to fire it, which they did with flax and hemp which they
brought out of the barn. . . . They fired it once, and one ventured out
and quenched it; but they quickly fired it again, and that took. Now
is the dreadful hour come that I have often heard of . . . but now mine
eyes see it. Some in our house were fighting for their lives, others
wallowing in their blood; the house on fire over our heads, and the
bloody heathen ready to knock us on the head if we stirred out. Now
might we hear mothers and children crying out for themselves and
one another, 'Lord, what shall we do?'

Then I took my children (and one of my sisters, hers) to go forth and
leave the house; but as soon as we came to the door and appeared, the
Indians shot so thick that the bullets rattled against the house as if one
had taken an handful of stones and threw them, so that we were fain
to give back. We had six stout dogs belonging to our garrison, but
none of them would stir, though another time, if any Indian had come
to the door, they were ready to fly upon him and tear him down. . . .
But out we must go, the fire increasing and coming along behind us
roaring, and the Indians gaping before us with their guns, spears, and
hatchets to devour us. No sooner were we out of the house but my
brother-in-law . . . fell down dead, whereat the Indians scornfully
shouted and hallowed, and were presently upon him, stripping off his
clothes. The bullets flying thick, one went through my side, and the
same (as would seem) through the bowels and hand of my dear child
in my arms. One of my eldest sister's children, named William [Kerley]
had then his leg broken, which the Indians perceiving, they knocked
him on head. . . . My eldest sister [Mrs. Kerley], being yet in the house

and seeing those woeful sights, . . . she said, 'And Lord, let me die with them!' Which was no sooner said but she was struck with a bullet and fell down dead over the threshold. . . . The Indians laid hold of us, pulling me one way and the children another, and said, 'Come, go along with us.' I told them they would kill me. They answered, if I were willing to go along with them, they would not hurt me. . . .

I had often before this said that, if the Indians should come, I should choose rather to be killed by them than taken alive; but when it came to the trial my mind changed; their glittering weapons so daunted my spirit, that I chose rather to go along with those (as I may say) ravenous beasts, than that moment to end my days. And that I may the better declare what happened to me during that grievous captivity, I shall particularly speak of the several removes we had up and down the wilderness. . . .

THE SECOND REMOVE

. . . After this it quickly began to snow. And when night came on they stopped; and now down I must sit in the snow, by a little fire and a few boughs behind me, with my sick child in my lap, and calling much for water, being now (through the wound) fallen into a violent fever; my own wound also growing so stiff that I could scarce sit down or rise up. . . . Still the Lord upheld me with His gracious and merciful spirit, and we were both alive to see the light of the next morning.

THE THIRD REMOVE

. . . Thus nine days I sat upon my knees, with my babe in my lap, till my flesh was raw again. My child, being even ready to depart this sorrowful world, they bade me carry it out to another wigwam (I suppose because they would not be troubled with such spectacles); whither I went with a very heavy heart, and down I sat with the picture of death in my lap. About two hours in the night, my sweet babe, like a lamb, departed this life, on Feb. 18, 1675. It being about six years and five months old. . . .

God having taken away this dear child, I went to see my daughter Mary, who was at this same Indian town, at a wigwam not very far off, though we had little liberty or opportunity to see one another. She was about ten years old, and taken from the door at first by a Praying Indian, and afterward sold for a gun. When I came in sight she would fall a-weeping, at which they were provoked and would not let me come near her, but bade me be gone, which was a heart-cutting word to me. I had one child dead, another in the wilderness I knew not where, the third they would not let me come near to. . . . Whereupon I earnestly entreated the Lord that He would consider my low estate and show me a token for good, and, if it were His blessed will, some sign and hope of some relief. And indeed quickly the Lord answered, in some measure, my poor prayers. For, as I was going up and down, mourning and lamenting my condition, my son came to me, and asked me how I did. I had not seen him before since the destruction of the town, and I knew not where he was till I was informed by himself that he was amongst a smaller parcel of Indians whose place was about six miles off. . . . I took this to be some gracious answer to my earnest and unfeigned desire.

The next day, *viz.* to this, the Indians returned from Medfield. . . . But before they came to us, oh, the outrageous roaring and hooping that there was! They began their din about a mile before they came to us. By their noise and hooping, they signified how many they had destroyed (which was at that time twenty-three). . . . And then, oh, the hideous insulting and triumphing that there was over some Englishmen's scalps that they had taken. . . .

I cannot but take notice of the wonderful mercy of God to me in those afflictions, in sending me a Bible. One of the Indians that came from Medfield fight had brought some plunder, came to me and asked me if I would have a Bible; he had got one in his basket. I was glad of it and asked him whether he thought the Indians would let me read. He answered, yes. So I took the Bible and, in that melancholy time it came into my mind to read first the 28th chapter of Deuteronomy, which I did. . . . But the Lord helped me still to go on reading till I came to chap. 30, the seven first verses, where I found there was mercy promised again, if we would return to him by repentance; and though we were scattered from one end of the earth to the other, yet the Lord would gather us together, and turn all those curses upon our enemies. I do not desire to live to forget this scripture, and what comfort it was to me. . . .

THE EIGHTH REMOVE

Then I went to see King Philip. He bade me come in and sit down, and asked me whether I would smoke it (an usual compliment now-a-days amongst saints and sinners). But this no way suited me; for, though I had formerly used tobacco, yet I had left it ever since I was first taken. It seems to be a bait the devil lays to make men lose their precious time. I remember with shame how, formerly, when I had taken two or three pipes, I was presently ready for another, such a bewitching thing it is. But I thank God He has now given me power over it. Surely there are many who may be better employed than to lie sucking a stinking tobacco-pipe. . . .

THE THIRTEENTH REMOVE

. . . I had not seen my son a pretty while, and here was an Indian of whom I made inquiry after him, and asked him when he saw him. He answered me that such a time his master roasted him, and that himself did eat a piece of him as big as his two fingers, and that he was very good meat. But the Lord upheld my spirit under this discouragement, and I considered their horrible addictedness to lying, and that there is not one of them that makes the least conscience of speaking of truth.

In this place, on a cold night, as I lay by the fire, I removed a stick that kept the heat from me. A squaw moved it down again, at which I looked up, and she threw an handful of ashes in mine eyes. I thought I should have been quite blinded and have never seen more; but, lying down, the water run out of my eyes and carried the dirt with it, that, by the morning, I recovered my sight again. . . .

THE TWENTIETH REMOVE

. . . On a Sabbath day, the sun being about an hour high in the afternoon, came Mr. John Hoar (the Council permitting him and his own forward spirit inclining him), together with the two forementioned Indians, Tom and Peter, with their third letter from the Council. . . . When they [the captor Indians] had talked their fill with him, they suffered me to go to him, We asked each other of our welfare, and how my husband did, and all my friends? He told me they were all well, and would be glad to see me. Amongst other things which my husband sent me, there came a pound of tobacco, which I sold for nine shillings in money. For many of the Indians, for want of tobacco, smoked hemlock and ground-ivy. It was a great mistake in any who thought I sent for tobacco; for, through the favour of God, that desire was overcome.

I now asked them whether I should go home with Mr. Hoar? They answered, No, one and another of them. . . . At night I asked them again if I should go home. They all as one said no, except my husband would come for me. When we were lain down, my master went out of the wigwam, and by and by sent in an Indian called James the Printer, who told Mr. Hoar that my master would let me go home tomorrow if he would let him have one pint of liquors. Then Mr. Hoar called his own Indians, Tom and Peter, and bid them go and see whether he would promise it before them three. And if he would, he should have it; which he did, and he had it. . . .

My master, after he had had his drink, quickly came ranting into the wigwam again, and called for Mr. Hoar, drinking to him and saying he was a good man; and then again he would say, 'Hang him, rogue.' . . . Then he called for me. I trembled to hear him, yet I was fain to go to him. And he drunk to me, showing no incivility. He was the first Indian I saw drunk all the while that I was amongst them. At last his squaw ran out, and he after her, round the wigwam, with his money jingling at his knees. But she escaped him. But, having an old squaw, he ran to her; and so, through the Lord's mercy, we were no more troubled with him that night. . . .

On Tuesday morning they called their General Court (as they call it) to consult and determine whether I should go home or no: and they all as one man did seemingly consent to it . . . except Philip, who would not come among them. . . . Where we may see a remarkable change of Providence: at first they were all against it, except my husband would come for me. But afterwards they assented to it, and seemed much to rejoice in it. Some asked me to send them some bread, others some tobacco, others shaking me by the hand, offering me a hood and scarf to ride in. . . . O the wonderful power of God that I have seen, and the experience that I have had: I have been in the midst of those roaring lions and savage bears, that feared neither God nor man, nor the devil, by night and day, alone and in company, sleeping all sorts together, and yet not one of them ever offered me the least abuse of unchastity to me, in word or action.

. . . Now was I full of joy, and yet not without sorrow. . . . [At Concord] I met with my brother, and my brother-in-law [Lt. Kerley], who asked me if I knew where his wife was. Poor heart! He had helped to bury her and knew it not. She, being shot down by the house, was partly burnt, so that those who were at Boston at the desolation of the town, and came back afterward and buried the dead, did not know her. . . .

About this time the Council had ordered a day of public thanksgiving, though I thought I had still cause of mourning. And, being unsettled in our minds, we thought we would ride toward the eastward, to see if we could hear anything concerning our children. And as we were riding along . . . we met with Mr. William Hubbard, who told us our son Joseph was come in to Major Waldren's, and another with him, which was my sister's son. . . . At night . . . one came and told him [Rev. Rowlandson] that his daughter was come in at Providence: here was mercy on both hands. Now hath God fulfilled that precious scripture, which was such a comfort to me in my distressed condition. . . .

Before I knew what affliction meant I was ready sometimes to wish for it. When I lived in prosperity, having the comforts of the world about me . . . and yet seeing many . . . under many trials and afflictions . . . I should be sometimes jealous least I should have my portion in this life; and that scripture would come to my mind, Heb. 12.6: 'For whom the Lord loveth he chasteneth, and scourgeth every son whom he receiveth.' But now I see the Lord had his time to scourge and chasten me. The portion of some is to have their affliction by drops, now one drop and then another. But the dregs of the cup, the wine of astonishment, like a sweeping rain that leaveth no food, did the Lord prepare to be my portion. . . .

Mary Rowlandson, *The Sovereignty and Goodness of God* (first printed Cambridge, Mass., 1682; no known copy of 1st ed. survives). London ed. with title *A True History of the Captivity . . . of Mrs. Mary Rowlandson* (1682), reprinted in Somers *Tracts*, ed. Walter Scott, viii (1812), pp. 557-82. Above excerpt based on 2nd Cambridge ed. (1682), reprinted in *Narratives of the Indian Wars* ('Orig. Narr.' series), ed. C. H. Lincoln (1913), pp. 112-67

5   A Virginian's View of the Indian Problem, 1705

Robert Beverley, the first native Virginian to write a history of the colony, was interested in the Indians and made a serious effort to understand their social attitudes and their religion. He suggested that intermarriage with the Indians might have helped to populate a barren land and to ensure a lasting peace.

Intermarriage had been indeed the method proposed very often by the Indians in the beginning, urging it frequently as a certain rule that the

English were not their friends if they refused it. And I can't but think it would have been happy for that country had they embraced this proposal: for, the jealousy of the Indians, which I take to be the cause of most of the rapines and murders they committed, would by this means have been altogether prevented, and consequently the abundance of blood that was shed on both sides would have been saved; the great extremities they were so often reduced to, by which so many died, would not have happened; the colony, instead of all these losses of men on both sides, would have been increasing in children to its advantage; the country would have escaped the odium which undeservedly fell upon it, by the errors and convulsions in the first management; and, in all likelihood, many, if not most, of the Indians would have been converted to Christianity by this kind method; the country would have been full of people, by the preservation of the many Christians and Indians that fell in the wars between them. Besides, there would have been a continuance of all those nations of Indians that are now dwindled away to nothing by their frequent removals, or are fled to other parts; not to mention the invitation that so much success and prosperity would have been for others to have gone over and settled there, instead of the frights and terrors that were produced by all those misfortunes that happened.

Pocahontas being thus married in the year 1613, a firm peace was concluded with her father, though he would not trust himself at her wedding. Both the English and Indians thought themselves entirely secure and quiet. This brought in the Chickahominy Indians also, though not out of any kindness or respect to the English, but out of fear of being, by their assistance, brought under Powhatan's absolute subjection, who used now and then to threaten and tyrannize over them. . . .

Though the young Indian women are said to prostitute their bodies for *wampum* . . . beads, and other such like fineries, yet I never could find any ground for the accusation and believe it only to be an unjust scandal upon them. This I know, that if ever they have a child while they are single, it is such a disgrace to them that they never after get husbands. Besides, I must do them the justice to say, I never heard of a child any of them had before marriage, and the Indians themselves disown any such custom; though they acknowledge at the same time that the maidens are entirely at their own disposal, and may manage their persons as they think fit. Indeed I believe this story to be an aspersion cast on those innocent creatures by reason of the freedom they take in conversation, which uncharitable Christians interpret as criminal, upon no other ground than the guilt of their own consciences.

The Indian damsels are full of spirit, and from thence are always inspired with mirth and good humor. They are extremely given to laugh, which they do with a grace not to be resisted. The excess of life and fire which they never fail to have makes them frolicsome, but without any real imputation to their innocence. However, this is ground enough for the English, who are not very nice in distinguishing between guilt and harmless freedom, to think them incontinent, though it be with as little justice as the jealous Spaniards condemn the liberty used by the women of France, which are much more chaste than their own ladies, which they keep under the strictest confinement.

The manner of the Indians treating their young children is very strange; for instead of keeping them warm at their first entry into the world, and wrapping them up with I don't know how many cloths, according to our fond custom, the first thing they do is to dip the child over head and ears in cold water, and then to bind it naked to a convenient board, having a hole fitly placed for evacuation; but they always put cotton, wool, fur, or other soft thing for the body to rest easy on, between the child and the board. In this posture they keep it several months, till the bones begin to harden, the joints to knit, and the limbs to grow strong; and then they let it loose from the board, suffering it to crawl about except when they are feeding or playing with it.

While the child is thus at the board they either lay it flat on its back or set it leaning on one end, or else hang it up by a string fastened to the upper end of the board for that purpose: the child and board being all this while carried about together. As our women undress their children to clean them and shift their linen, so they do theirs to wash and grease them.

The method the women have of carrying their children after they are suffered to crawl about is very particular; they carry them at their backs in summer, taking one leg of the child under their arm, and the counter-arm of the child in their hand over their shoulder; the other leg hanging down, and the child all the while holding fast with its other hand; but in winter they carry them in the hollow of their match-coat at their back, leaving nothing but the child's head out. . . .

Once in my travels, in very cold weather, I met at an Englishman's house with an Indian of whom an extraordinary character had been given me for his ingenuity and understanding. When I see he had no other Indian with him, I thought I might be the more free; and therefore I made much of him, seating him close by a large fire and giving him plenty of strong cider, which I hoped would make him good company and openhearted. After I found him well warmed (for unless they be surprised some way or other they will not talk freely of their religion), I asked him concerning their god, and what their notions of him were? He freely told me, they believed God was universally beneficent, that His dwelling was in the heavens above, and that the influences of His goodness reached to the earth beneath. That He was incomprehensible in His excellence, and enjoyed all possible felicity; that His duration was eternal, His perfection boundless, and that He possesses everlasting indolence and ease. I told him I had heard that they worshipped the devil, and asked why they did not rather worship God, whom they had so high an opinion of and who would give them all good things and protect them from any mischief that the devil could do them? To this his answer was that, 'tis true, God is the giver of all good things, but they flow naturally and promiscuously from him; that they are showered down upon all men indifferently without distinction; that God does not trouble himself with the impertinent affairs of men, nor is concerned at what they do; but leaves them to make the most of their free will and to secure as many as they can of the good things that flow from Him. That therefore it was to no purpose either to fear or worship Him. But on the contrary, if they did not pacify the Evil Spirit and make him propitious, he would take away or spoil all those good things that God had given and ruin their health, their peace and their plenty by sending war, plague, and famine among them; for, said he, this Evil Spirit is always busying himself with our affairs and frequently visiting us, being present in the air, in the thunder, and in the storms. He told me farther that he expected adoration and sacrifice from them, on pain of his displeasure; and that therefore they thought it convenient to make their court to him. I then asked him concerning the image which they worship in their *Quioccasan*, and assured him that it was a dead insensible log equipped with a bundle of clouts, a mere helpless thing made by men that could neither hear, see, nor speak; and that such a stupid thing could no ways hurt or help them. To this he answered very unwillingly and with much hesitation; however, he at last delivered himself in these broken and imperfect sentences: 'It is the priests – they make the people believe, and –' here he paused a little and then repeated to me that it was the priests –. And then gave me hopes that he would have said something more, but a qualm crossed

his conscience and hindered him from making any farther confession.
. . .

The solemnity of *Huskanawing* is commonly practised once every four-teen or sixteen years, or oftener, as their young men happen to grow up. It is an institution or discipline which all young men must pass before they can be admitted to be of the number of the great men, or *Cocka-rouses* [Council members] of the nation; whereas by Captain Smith's relation they were only set apart to supply the priesthood. The whole ceremony is performed after the following manner:

The choicest and briskest young men of the town, and such only as have acquired some treasure by their travels and hunting, are chosen out by the rulers to be *Huskanawed*; and whoever refuses to undergo this process, dare not remain among them. Several of those odd pre-paratory fopperies are premised in the beginning which have been before related; but the principal part of the business is to carry them into the woods and there keep them, under confinement and destitute of all society, for several months, giving them no other sustenance but the infusion, on decoction, of some poisonous intoxicating roots; by virtue of which physic, and by the severity of the discipline which they undergo, they become stark staring mad; in which raving condition they are kept eighteen or twenty days. During these extremities they are shut up, night and day, in a strong enclosure made on purpose; one of which I saw, belonging to the Pamunkey Indians, in the year 1694. It was in shape like a sugar-loaf and every way open like a lattice for the air to pass through. . . . In this cage thirteen young men had been *Huskanawed*, and had not been a month set at liberty when I saw it. Upon this occasion it is pretended that these poor creatures drink so much of that water of *Lethe* that they perfectly lose the remembrance of all former things, even of their parents, their treasure, and their language. When the doctors find that they have drank sufficiently of the *Wysoccan* (so they call this mad potion) they gradually restore them to their senses again by lessening the intoxication of their diet. But be-fore they are perfectly well they bring them back into their towns while they are still wild and crazy through the violence of the medicine. After this they are very fearful of discovering anything of their former remembrance; for if such a thing should happen to any of them, they must immediately be *Huskanawed* again; and the second time the usage is so severe that seldom anyone escapes with life. Thus they must pre-tend to have forgot the very use of their tongues, so as not to be able to speak nor understand anything that is spoken, till they learn it again.

Now whether this be real or counterfeit, I don't know; but certain it is that they will not for some time take notice of anybody nor anything with which they were before acquainted, being still under the guard of their keepers, who constantly wait upon them everywhere till they have learnt all things perfectly over again. Thus they unlive their former lives and commence men by forgetting that they ever have been boys. If under this exercise anyone should die, I suppose the story of *Okee*, mentioned by Smith, is the salvo for it: For (says he) *Okee* was to have such as were his by lot; and such were said to be sacrificed.

Now this conjecture is the more probable because we know that *Okee* has not a share in every *Huskanawing*; for though two young men happened to come short home, in that of the Pamunkey Indians which was performed in the year 1694, yet the Appomattocs, formerly a great nation though now an inconsiderable people, made an *Huskanaw* in the year 1690 and brought home the same number they carried out.

I can account no other way for the great pains and secrecy of the keepers, during the whole process of this discipline, but by assuring you that it is the most meritorious thing in the world to discharge that trust well in order to their preferment to the greatest posts in the nation, which they claim as their undoubted right in the next promotion. On the other hand, they are sure of a speedy passport into the other world if they should by their levity or neglect show themselves in the least unfaithful.

Those which I ever observed to have been *Huskanawed* were lively, handsome, well-timbered young men from fifteen to twenty years of age or upward, and such as were generally reputed rich. I confess I judged it at first sight to be only an invention of the seniors to engross the young men's riches to themselves. For, after suffering this operation they never pretended to call to mind anything of their former property; but their goods were either shared among the old men or brought to some public use; and so those younkers were obliged to begin the world again.

But the Indians detest this opinion, and pretend that this violent method of taking away the memory is to release the youth from all their childish impressions and from that strong partiality to persons and things which is contracted before reason comes to take place. They hope by this proceeding to root out all the prepossessions and unreasonable prejudices which are fixed in the minds of children. So that, when the young men come to themselves again, their reason may act freely without being biased by the cheats of custom and education. Thus also they become discharged from the remembrance of any ties by blood, and are established in a state of equality and perfect freedom to order their actions and dispose of their persons as they think fit, without any other control than that of the law of nature. By this means also they become qualified, when they have any public office, equally and impartially to administer justice, without having respect either to friend or relation.

> Robert Beverley, *The History and Present State of Virginia* (1705), ed. L. B. Wright (1947), pp. 38-9, 170-3, 200-1, 207-9

VII

PEOPLE AND CONDITIONS OF LIFE

1 Sir Thomas Gates' Low Opinion of His Colonists, 1610

Sir Thomas Gates, who commanded the *Sea Venture* in the ill-fated expedition of 1609 that wrecked in Bermuda, arrived in Virginia in the spring of 1610 at the end of the 'starving time'. So destitute were the surviving colonists that Gates recommended abandonment of the colony. On their way down Chesapeake Bay the settlers met a fresh expedition led by Lord De La Warr, who returned them to Jamestown. The following account is based on Gates' report of the quality of the colonists and their difficulties.

The next fountain of woes was secure negligence and improvidence, when every man sharked for his present booty but was altogether careless of succeeding penury. Now I demand whether Sicilia or Sardinia (sometimes the barns of Rome) could hope for increase without manuring? A colony is therefore denominated because they should be *coloni*, the tillers of the earth and stewards of fertility. Our mutinous loiterers would not sow with providence, and therefore they reaped the fruits of too dear-bought repentance. An incredible example of their idleness is the report of Sir Thomas Gates, who affirmeth that, after his first coming thither, he had seen some of them eat their fish raw rather than they would go a stone's cast to fetch wood and dress it. *Dei laboribus omnia vendunt*, God sells us all things for our labour, when Adam himself might not live in paradise without dressing the garden.

Unto idleness you may join treasons, wrought by those unhallowed creatures that forsook the colony and exposed their desolate brethren to extreme misery. You shall know that 28 or 30 of the company were appointed (in the ship called the *Swallow*) to truck for corn with the

Indians; and having obtained a great quantity by trading, the most seditious of them conspired together, persuaded some & enforced others to this barbarous project: they stole away the ship, they made a league amongst themselves to be professed pirates, with dream of mountains of gold and happy robberies. Thus at one instant they wronged the hopes and subverted the cares of the colony who depended upon their return, fore-slowed to look out for further provision; they created the Indians our implacable enemies by some violence they had offered; they carried away the best ship (which should have been a refuge in extremities); they weakened our forces by substraction of their arms and succours. These are that scum of men that, failing in their piracy, that, being pinched with famine and penury after their wild roving upon the sea, when all their lawless hopes failed some remained with other pirates they met upon the sea; the others, resolved to return to England, bound themselves by mutual oath to agree all in one report: to discredit the land, to deplore the famine, and to protest that this their coming away proceeded from desperate necessity. . . .

Unto treasons you may join covetousness in the mariners who, for their private lucre, partly embezzled the provisions, partly prevented our trade with the Indians, making the matches in the night and forestalling our market in the day, whereby the Virginians were glutted with our trifles and enhanced the prices of their corn and victual. . . .

Join unto these another evil: there is great store of fish in the river, especially of sturgeon; but our men provided no more of them than for present necessity, not barreling up any store against that season the sturgeon returned to the sea. And not to dissemble their folly, they suffered fourteen nets (which was all they had) to rot and spoil which, by orderly drying and mending, might have been preserved but, being lost, all help of fishing perished. . . .

The state of the colony by these accidents began to find a sensible declining, which Powhatan (as a greedy vulture) observing, and boiling with desire of revenge, he invited Captain Ratcliffe and about thirty others to trade for corn; and under the colour of fairest friendship he brought them within the compass of his ambush, whereby they were cruelly murdered and massacred. . . .

Cast up this reckoning together: want of government, store of idleness, their expectations frustrated by the traitors, their market spoiled by the mariners, our nets broken, the deer chased, our boats lost, our hogs killed, our trade with the Indians forbidden, some of our men fled, some murdered, and most by drinking of the brackish water of James fort weakened and indangered, famine and sickness by all these means increased, here at home the monies came in so slowly that the Lord [De] La Warr could not be dispatched till the colony was worn and spent with difficulties. Above all, having neither ruler nor preacher, they neither feared God nor man, which provoked the wrath of the Lord of Hosts and pulled down His judgements upon them.

> *A True Declaration of the Estate of the Colony in Virginia* (1610), reprinted in *Tracts*, etc., ed. P. Force (1947), iii.15-18

2   Thanksgiving at Plymouth Plantation, 1621, 1623

The colonists from time to time celebrated days of thanksgiving. A natural time was the gathering-in of the harvest, a tradition probably remembered from harvest festivals in England. In modern times a national holiday, known as Thanksgiving Day, has become established on the last Thursday in November.

[September 1621]
They began now to gather in the small harvest they had, and to fit up their houses and dwellings against winter, being all well recovered in health and strength and had all things in good plenty. For as some were thus employed in affairs abroad, others were exercised in fishing, about cod and bass and other fish, of which they took good store, of which every family had their portion. All the summer there was no want; and now began to come in store of fowl, as winter approached, of which this place did abound when they came first (but afterward decreased by degrees). And besides waterfowl there was great store of wild turkeys, of which they took many, besides venison, etc. Besides they had about a peck a meal a week to a person, or now since harvest, Indian corn to that proportion. Which made many afterwards write so largely of their plenty here to their friends in England, which were not feigned but true reports.

[July? 1623] . . . Notwithstanding all their great pains and industry and the great hopes of a large crop, the Lord seemed to blast and take away the same, and to threaten further and more sore famine unto them by a great drought which continued from the 3rd week in May till about the middle of July, without any rain and with great heat . . .

insomuch as the corn began to wither away, though it was set with fish, the moisture whereof helped it much. . . . Upon which they set apart a solemn day of humiliation to seek the Lord by humble and fervent prayer in this great distress. And He was pleased to give them a gracious and speedy answer, both to their own and the Indians' admiration that lived amongst them. For all the morning and greatest part of the day it was clear weather and very hot and not a cloud or any sign of rain to be seen, yet toward evening it began to overcast and shortly after to rain, with such sweet and gentle showers as gave them cause of rejoicing and blessing God. It came without either wind or thunder or any violence, and by degrees in that abundance as that the earth was thoroughly wet and soaked therewith. Which did so apparently revive and quicken the decayed corn and other fruits as was wonderful to see and made the Indians astonished to behold. And afterwards the Lord sent them such seasonable showers, with interchange of fair warm weather, as . . . caused a fruitful and liberal harvest. . . . For which mercy (in time convenient) they also set apart a day of thanksgiving.

Of Plymouth Plantation. See Morison ed., pp. 90, 131–2

3 Observations on Colonial Life, 1705

Robert Beverley, in his *History and Present State of Virginia*, provides much detailed information about the way of life that had developed in the oldest of the English colonies by the beginning of the eighteenth century.

OF THE PEOPLE, INHABITANTS OF VIRGINIA

I can easily imagine . . . that this, as well as all the rest of the plantations, was for the most part at first peopled by persons of low circumstances and by such as were willing to seek their fortunes in a foreign country. Nor was it likely that any man of a plentiful estate should voluntarily abandon a happy certainty to roam after imaginary advantages in a New World. . . .

Those that went over to that country first were chiefly single men who had not the encumbrance of wives and children in England; and if they had they did not expose them to the fatigue and hazard of so long a voyage until they saw how it should fare with themselves. From hence it came to pass that when they were settled there in a comfortable way of subsisting a family they grew sensible of the misfortune of wanting wives, and such as had left wives in England sent for them; but the single men were put to their shifts. They excepted against the Indian women on account of their being pagans, and for fear they should conspire with those of their own nation to destroy their husbands. Under this difficulty they had no hopes but that the plenty in which they lived might invite modest women of small fortunes to go over thither from England. However, they would not receive any but such as could carry sufficient certificate of their modesty and good behaviour. Those, if they were but moderately qualified in all other respects, might depend upon marrying very well in those days without any fortune. Nay, the first planters were so far from expecting money with a woman that 'twas a common thing for them to buy a deserving wife at the price of 100 pound, and make themselves believe they had a hopeful bargain.

But this way of peopling the colony was only at first. For after the advantages of the climate and the fruitfulness of the soil were well known, and all the dangers incident to infant settlements were over, people of better condition retired thither with their families, either to increase the estates they had before, or else to avoid being persecuted for their principles of religion or government. Thus in the time of the Rebellion in England, several good Cavalier families went thither with their effects to escape the tyranny of the usurper. And so again, upon the Restoration, many people of the opposite party took refuge there to shelter themselves from the King's resentment. But they had not many of these last, because that country [Virginia] was famous for holding out the longest for the royal family of any of the English dominions. For which reason the Roundheads went for the most part to New England, as did most of those that, in the reign of King Charles II, were molested on the account of their religion, though some of these fell likewise to the share of Virginia. As for malefactors condemned to transportation, they have always received very few, and for many years last past their laws have been severe against them. . . .

That which makes this country most unfortunate is that it must submit to receive its character from the mouths not only of unfit but very unequal judges. For all its reproaches happen after this manner: Many of the merchants and others that go thither from England make no distinction between a cold and a hot country; but wisely go sweltering about in their thick clothes all the summer because they used to do so in their northern climate; and then unfairly complain of the heat of the country. They greedily surfeit with their delicious fruits and are guilty of great intemperance through the exceeding generosity of the inhabitants; by which means they fall sick and then unjustly complain of the unhealthiness of the country.

Beverley, *History and Present State*, ed. Wright, pp. 286–97

4 The Journey of Sarah Knight from Boston to New York, 1704–1705

Sarah Kemble Knight (1666–1727), a Boston school teacher, was also employed in business and legal affairs. She was the daughter of a merchant and wife of a shipmaster, Captain Richard Knight, a widower considerably older than herself. Some sort of business, possibly the settlement of an estate, took her to New York in 1704, a time when travel was difficult and dangerous for men and unheard of for an unescorted woman. Madam Knight, however, was a woman of spirit as the journal of her trip makes clear.

Monday, October the second, 1704. About three o'clock afternoon I begun my journey from Boston to New Haven, being about two hundred mile. My kinsman, Captain Robert Luist, waited on me as far as Dedham, where I was to meet the western post.

I visited the Reverd. Mr. Belcher, the minister of the town, and tarried there till evening in hopes the post would come along. But he not coming, I resolved to go to Billings's, where he used to lodge, being 12 miles further. But being ignorant of the way, Madam Belcher, seeing no persuasions of her good spouse's or hers could prevail with me to lodge there that night, very kindly went with me to the tavern, where I hoped to get my guide, and desired the hostess to inquire of her guests whether any of them would go with me. But they being tied by the lips to a pewter engine, scarcely allowed themselves time ... [Part of MS missing. Apparently, the guests being unwilling, the hostess offered the services of her son John for several 'pieces of eight'.]

I told her no, I would not be accessary to such extortion.

'Then John shan't go,' says she, 'No indeed, shan't he.' And held forth at that rate a long time, that I began to fear I was got among the quaking tribe, believing not a limber-tongued sister among them could outdo Madam Hostess.

Upon this, to my no small surprise, son John arose and gravely demanded what I would give him to go with me.

'Give you?' says I. 'Are you John?'

'Yes,' says he, 'for want of a better.' And behold! this John looked as old as my host, and perhaps had been a man in the last century.

'Well, Mr. John,' says I, 'make your demands.'

'Why, half a piece of eight and a dram,' says John.

I agree and gave him a dram (now) in hand to bind the bargain.

My hostess catechised John for going so cheap, saying his poor wife would break her heart. . . .

His shade on his horse resembled a globe on a gate post. His habit, horse, and furniture, its looks and goings, incomparably answered the rest. Thus jogging on with an easy pace, my guide telling me it was dangerous to ride hard in the night (which his horse had the sense to avoid), he entertained me with the adventures he had passed by late riding, and eminent dangers he had escaped so that, remembering the heroes in *Parismus* and the *Knight of the Oracle*, I didn't know but I had met with a prince disguised.

When we had rid about an hour we come into a thick swamp which, by reason of a great fog, very much startled me, it being now very dark. But nothing dismayed John: he had encountered a thousand and a thousand such swamps, having a universal knowledge in the woods; and readily answered all my inquiries, which were not a few.

In about an hour . . . after we left the swamp we come to Billings's, where I was to lodge. My guide dismounted and very complaisantly helped me down and showed the door, signing to me with his hand to go in, which I gladly did. But had not gone many steps into the room ere I was interrogated by a young lady I understood afterwards was the eldest daughter of the family, with these, or words to this purpose, viz.:

'Law for me! What in the world brings you here at this time a night? I never see a woman on the road so dreadful late in all the days of my versal life. Who are you? Where are you going? I'm scared out of my wits!' – with much more of the same kind. I stood aghast, preparing to reply, when in comes my guide. To him Madam turned, roaring out:

'Lawful heart, John, is it you? How de do! Where in the world are you going with this woman? Who is she?'

John made no ansr. but sat down in the corner, fumbled out his black junk [bottle] and saluted that instead of Deb. She then turned again to me and fell anew into her silly questions, without asking me to sit down.

I told her she treated me very rudely and I did not think it my duty to answer her unmannerly questions. . . . I paid honest John with money and dram according to contract and dismissed him, and prayed Miss to show me where I must lodge. She conducted me to a parlour in a little back lean-to, which was almost filled with the bedstead which was so high that I was forced to climb on a chair to get up to the wretched bed that lay on it; on which, having stretched my tired limbs and laid my head on a sad-coloured pillow, I began to think on the transactions of the past day.

Tuesday, October the third, about 8 in the morning, I with the post proceeded forward without observing anything remarkable; and about two, afternoon, arrived at the post's second stage, where the western post met him and exchanged letters. Here, having called for something to eat, the woman brought in a twisted thing like a cable, but something whiter; and, laying it on the board, tugged for life to bring it into a capacity to spread; which having with great pains accomplished, she served in a dish of pork and cabbage, I suppose the remains of dinner. The sauce was of a deep purple, which I thought was boiled in her dye kettle. The bread was Indian, and everything on the table service agreeable to these. I, being hungry, got a little down. But my stomach was soon cloyed, and what cabbage I swallowed served me for a cud the whole day after. . . .

Being come to Mr. Havens's, I was very civilly received and courteously entertained in a clean, comfortable house. . . . But I could get no sleep because of the clamour of some of the town topers in next room, who were entered into a strong debate concerning the signification of the name of their country, viz. *Narraganset*. One said it was named so by the Indians because there grew a brier there of a prodigious height and bigness, the like hardly ever known, called by the Indians Narraganset. And quotes an Indian of so barbarous a name, for his author, that I could not write it. His antagonist replied no, it was from a spring it had its name, which he well knew where it was, which was extreme cold in summer and as hot as could be imagined in the winter, which was much resorted to by the natives, and by them called Narraganset (hot and cold), and that was the original of their place's name – with a thousand impertinences not worth notice, which he uttered with such a roaring voice and thundering blows with the fist of wickedness on the table that it pierced my very head. I heartily fretted and wished 'um tongue-tied, but with as little success as a friend of mine once who was, as she said, kept a whole night awake, on a journey, by a country Left. and a Sergeant, Insigne, and a Deacon contriving how to bring a triangle into a square. . . .

Wednesday, October 4th. About four in the morning we set out for Kingston . . . with a French doctor in our company. He and the post put on very furiously so that I could not keep up with them, only as now and then they'd stop till they see me. This road was poorly furnished with accomodations for travellers, so that we were forced to ride 22 miles by the post's account, but nearer thirty by mine, before we could bait so much as our horses, which I exceedingly complained of. But the post encouraged me by saying we should be well accommodated anon at Mr. Devil's a few miles further. But I questioned whether we ought to go to the Devil to be helped out of affliction. However, like the rest of deluded souls that post to the infernal den, we made all possible speed to this Devil's habitation. Where alighting, in full assurance of good accommodation we were going in. But meeting his two daughters – as I supposed twins, they so nearly resembled each other both in features and habit, and looked as old as the Devil himself and quite as ugly – we desired entertainment. But could hardly get a word out of 'um till, with our importunity, telling them our necessity, etc., they called the old Sophister; who was as sparing of his words as his daughters had been and no, or none, was the replies he made us to our demands. He differed only in this from the old fellow in tother country: he let us depart. . . .

There are everywhere in the towns as I passed a number of Indians, the natives of the country, and are the most savage of all the savages of that kind that I had ever seen, little or no care taken (as I heard upon inquiry) to make them otherwise. They have in some places lands of their own, and governed by laws of their own making. They marry many wives and at pleasure put them away – and on the least dislike or fickle humour, on either side; saying 'Stand away' to one another is a sufficient divorce. . . .

Being at a merchant's house, in comes a tall country fellow with his alforges full of tobacco; for they seldom loose their cud, but keep chewing and spitting as long as their eyes are open. He advanced to the middle of the room, makes an awkward nod and, spitting a large deal of aromatic tincture, he gave a scrape with his shovel-like shoe, leaving a small shovel-full of dirt on the floor, made a full stop, hugging his own pretty body with his hands under his arms, stood staring round him like a cat let out of a basket. At last, like the creature Balaam rode on, he opened his mouth and said: 'Have you any ribbonen for hat-bands to sell I pray?'

The questions and answers about the pay being past, the ribbon is brought and opened. Bumpkin simpers, cries 'It's confounded gay, I vow,' and beckoning to the door, in comes Joan Tawdry dropping about 50 curtsies and stands by him. He shows her the ribbon.

'Law, you,' says she, 'it's right gent. Do you take it, 'tis dreadful pretty.' . . .

The city of New York is a pleasant, well compacted place, situated on a commodious river which is a fine harbour for shipping. The buildings brick generally, very stately and high, though not altogether like ours in Boston. The bricks in some of the houses are of divers colours and, laid in checkers, being glazed look very agreeable. The inside of them are neat to admiration. . . .

They have vendues very frequently and make their earnings very well by them, for they treat with good liquor liberally, and the customers drink as liberally and generally pay for't as well by paying for that which they bid up briskly for, after the sack has gone plentifully about – tho' sometimes good pennyworths are got there.

Their diversions in the winter is riding sleighs about three or four miles out of town, where they have houses of entertainment at a place called the Bowery. . . . I believe we met 50 or 60 sleighs that day – they fly with great swiftness and some are so furious that they'll turn out of the path for none except a loaden cart. . . .

Saturday, Dec. 23, a very cold and windy day, after an intolerable night's lodging, we hasted forward. . . . Having rid thro a difficult river we come to Fairfield. . . . This is a considerable town and filled, as they say, with wealthy people; have a spacious meeting house and good buildings. But the inhabitants are litigious, nor do they well agree with their minister who (they say) is a very worthy gentleman. They have abundance of sheep, whose very dung brings them great gain; with part of which they pay their parson's salary. And they grudge that, prefering their dung before their minister. They let out their sheep at so much as they agree upon for a night. The highest bidder always carries them. And they will sufficiently dung a large quantity of land before morning. But were once bit by a sharper who had them a night and sheared them all before morning. . . .

Now it grew late in the afternoon and, the people having very much discouraged us about the sloughy way which they said we should find very difficult and hazardous, it so wrought on me, being tired and dispirited and disappointed of my desires of going home, that I agreed to lodge there that night, which we did at the house of one Draper. And the next day, being March 3rd, we got safe home to Boston.

Diary first published in *The Journals of Madam Knight and Rev. Mr. Buckingham*, ed. Timothy Dwight (1825), reprinted *The Private Journal of Sarah Kemble Knight*, ed. R. P. Keep (1901), pp. 27-75 *passim*

5   The Daily Life of a Virginia Grandee, 1711

William Byrd II was one of the most ornamental of the colonial gentry. He represented the colony of Virginia on numerous occasions as official agent in England. When in Virginia he took an active part in the political and social life of the colony. A secret diary that he kept in shorthand gives vivid glimpses of the activities of a man of his class in the early eighteenth century.

[Feb.] 4. I rose at 5 o'clock and read a chapter in Hebrew and some Greek in Lucian. I said my prayers and ate boiled milk for breakfast. I gave my necessary orders to Tom Turpin and he went away about 10 o'clock. About 11 we walked to church and heard a good sermon of Mr. Anderson. After church we ate some toast and drank some mead and went over the creek with our horses where the water was very high and I was very wet and got a violent cold. Mrs. Dunn returned home and we rode to my brother Duke's where we found all well. My sister did not ask us to eat till my brother came home and then I got some milk and potatoes. My cold grew worse. About 9 o'clock we went to bed. I said a short prayer and had good thoughts, good humor, and indifferent good health, thank God Almighty.

5. I rose about 8 o'clock and found my cold still worse. I said my prayers and ate milk and potatoes for breakfast. My wife and I quarreled

about her pulling her brows. She threatened she would not go to Williamsburg if she might not pull them; I refused, however, and got the better of her, and maintained my authority. About 10 o'clock we went over the river and got to Colonel Duke's about 11. There I ate some toast and canary. Then we proceeded to Queen's Creek, where we found all well, thank God. We ate roast goose for supper. The women prepared to go to the Governor's the next day and my brother and I talked of old stories. My cold grew exceedingly bad so that I thought I should be sick. My sister gave me some sage tea and leaves of [s-m-n-k] which made me mad all night so that I could not sleep but was much disordered by it. I neglected to say my prayers in form but had good thoughts, good humor, and indifferent health, thank God Almighty.

6. I rose about 9 o'clock but was so bad I thought I should not have been in condition to go to Williamsburg, and my wife was so kind to [say] she would stay with me, but rather than keep her from going I resolved to go if possible. I was shaved with a very dull razor, and ate some boiled milk for breakfast but neglected to say my prayers. About 10 o'clock I went to Williamsburg without the ladies. As soon as I got there it began to rain, which hindered about [sic] the company from coming. I went to the President's where I drank tea and went with him to the Governor's and found him at home. Several gentlemen were there and about 12 o'clock several ladies came. My wife and her sister came about 2. We had a short Council but more for form than for business. There was no other appointed in the room of Colonel Digges. My cold was a little better so that I ventured among the ladies, and Colonel Carter's wife and daughter were among them. It was night before we went to supper, which was very fine and in good order. It rained so that several did not come that were expected. About 7 o'clock the company went in coaches from the Governor's house to the capitol where the Governor opened the ball with a French dance with my wife. Then I danced with Mrs. Russel and then several others and among the rest Colonel Smith's son, who made a sad freak. Then we danced country dances for an hour and the company was carried into another room where was a very fine collation of sweetmeats. The Governor was very gallant to the ladies and very courteous to the gentlemen. About 2 o'clock the company returned in the coaches and because the drive was dirty the Governor carried the ladies into their coaches. My wife and I lay at my lodgings. Colonel Carter's family and Mr. Blair were stopped by the unruliness of the horses and Daniel Wilkinson was

so gallant as to lead the horses himself through all the dirt and rain to Mr. Blair's house. My cold continued bad. I neglected to say my prayers and had good thoughts, good humor, but indifferent health, thank God Almighty. It rained all day and all night. The President had the worst clothes of anybody there.

7. I rose at 8 o'clock and found my cold continued. I said my prayers and ate boiled milk for breakfast. I went to see Mr. Clayton who lay sick of the gout. About 11 o'clock my wife and I went to wait on the Governor in the President's coach. We went there to take our leave but were forced to stay all day. The Governor had made a bargain with his servants that if they would forbear to drink upon the Queen's birthday, they might be drunk this day. They observed their contract and did their business very well and got very drunk today, in such a manner that Mrs. Russell's maid was forced to lay the cloth, but the cook in that condition made a shift to send in a pretty little dinner. I ate some mutton cutlets. In the afternoon I persuaded my wife to stay all night in town and so it was resolved to spend the evening in cards. My cold was very bad and I lost my money. About 10 o'clock the Governor's coach carried us home to our lodgings where my wife was out of humor and I out of order. I said a short prayer and had good thoughts and good humor, thank God Almighty.

8. I rose at 7 o'clock and we both got ready to go. I said my prayers and ate boiled milk for breakfast. We expected the Governor at my lodgings and he came about 9 o'clock. We stayed there a little while and then I walked with him to the house that is building for the Governor where he showed me abundance of faults and found great exception to the proceedings of the workmen. The Governor was pleased to tell me his thoughts about the auditor's place and told me several had made application for it and that one gentleman (that I took to be Holloway) had offered £500 for it. The Governor assisted my wife to get on her horse and then we took leave and rode to Mr. Blair's where we had some milk tea. Then we proceeded to Colonel Duke's where I got 50 black cherry trees for the Governor. We ate some boiled beef for dinner and then sat and talked all the evening. I neglected to say my prayers but had good thoughts, good humor, and indifferent good health, thank God Almighty.

The Secret Diary of William Byrd of Westover,
1709-1712, eds, L. B. Wright and M. Tinling
(1941), pp. 296-9

6 Benjamin Franklin Travels from New York to Philadelphia, 1723

Benjamin Franklin learned the printer's trade in Boston as apprentice to his half brother, James, publisher of *The New England Courant*. Chafing under the master-apprentice relationship within the family, Benjamin quit his brother's service to seek employment in New York. The printer there, 'having little to do', told him of a possible opening in Philadelphia. Franklin's autobiography gives the following account of travel between the two cities in 1723.

The inclination I had had for the sea was by this time done away, or I might now have gratified it. But having another profession and conceiving myself a pretty good workman, I offered my services to the printer of the place, old Mr. Wm. Bradford (who had been the first printer in Pennsylvania, but had removed thence in consequence of a quarrel with the Governor, Geo. Keith). He could give me no employment, having little to do and hands enough already. 'But,' says he, 'my son at Philadelphia has lately lost his principal hand, Aquila Rose, by death. If you go thither I believe he may employ you.'

Philadelphia was a hundred miles farther. I set out, however, in a boat for Amboy, leaving my chest and things to follow me round by sea. In crossing the bay we met with a squall that tore our rotten sails to pieces, prevented our getting into the kill, and drove us upon Long Island. In our way a drunken Dutchman, who was a passenger too, fell overboard; when he was sinking, I reached through the water to his shock pate and drew him up so that we got him in again. His ducking sobered him a little and he went to sleep, taking first out of his pocket a book which he desired I would dry for him. It proved to be my old favourite author Bunyan's *Pilgrim's Progress* in Dutch, finely printed on good paper with copper cuts, a dress better than I had ever seen it wear in its own language. I have since found that it has been translated into most of the languages of Europe, and suppose it has been more generally read than any other book except, perhaps, the Bible. Honest John was the first that I know of who mixes narration and dialogue, a method of writing very engaging to the reader, who in the most interesting parts finds himself, as it were, admitted into the company and present at the conversation. Defoe has imitated him successfully in his *Robinson Crusoe*, in his *Moll Flanders*, and other pieces; and Richardson has done the same in his *Pamela*, etc.

On approaching the island, we found it was in a place where there could be no landing, there being a great surf on the stony beach. So we dropped anchor and swung out our cable towards the shore. Some people came down to the water edge and hallooed to us, as we did to them, but the wind was so high and the surf so loud that we could not understand each other. There were some canoes on the shore, and we made signs and called to them to fetch us, but they either did not comprehend us or thought it impracticable, so they went off. Night approaching, we had no remedy but to have patience till the wind abated, and in the meantime the boatman and I concluded to sleep if we could, and so we crowded into the scuttle with the Dutchman who was still wet, and the spray breaking over the head of our boat leaked through to us so that we were soon almost as wet as he. In this manner we lay all night with very little rest; but, the wind abating the next day, we made a shift to reach Amboy before night, having been thirty hours on the water without victuals or any drink but a bottle of filthy rum, the water we sailed on being salt.

In the evening I found myself very feverish and went to bed; but, having read somewhere that cold water drank plentifully was good for a fever, I followed the prescription, sweat plentifully most of the night, my fever left me, and, in the morning crossing the ferry, I proceeded on my journey on foot, having fifty miles to Burlington where I was told I should find boats that would carry me the rest of the way to Philadelphia.

It rained very hard all the day, I was thoroughly soaked and by noon a good deal tired, so I stopped at a poor inn where I stayed all night, beginning now to wish I had never left home. I made so miserable a figure, too, that I found by the questions asked me I was suspected to be some runaway servant and in danger of being taken up on that suspicion. However, I proceeded the next day and got in the evening to an inn within eight or ten miles of Burlington, kept by one Dr. Brown.

He entered into conversation with me while I took some refreshment and, finding I had read a little, became very sociable and friendly. Our acquaintance continued all the rest of his life. He had been, I imagine, an itinerant doctor, for there was no town in England or any country in Europe of which he could not give a very particular account. He had some letters and was ingenious, but he was an infidel and wickedly undertook some years after to travesty the Bible in doggerel verse as Cotton had done with Virgil. By this means he set many of the facts in a very ridiculous light and might have done mischief with weak minds if his work had been published, but it never was. At his house I lay that night, and the next morning reached Burlington, but had the mortification to find that the regular boats were gone a little before and no other expected to go before Tuesday, this being Saturday. Wherefore I returned to an old woman in the town of whom I had bought some gingerbread to eat on the water and asked her advice; she invited me to lodge at her house till a passage by water should offer and, being tired with my foot travelling, I accepted the invitation. Understanding I was a printer, she would have had me remain in that town and follow my business, being ignorant of the stock necessary to begin with. She was very hospitable, gave me a dinner of ox cheek with great goodwill, accepting only of a pot of ale in return. And I thought myself fixed till Tuesday should come. However, walking in the evening by the side of the river, a boat came by which I found was going towards Philadelphia with several people in her. They took me in and, as there was no wind, we rowed all the way; and about midnight, not having yet seen the city, some of the company were confident we must have passed it and would row no farther; the others knew not where we were, so we put towards the shore, got into a creek, landed near an old fence, with the rails of which we made a fire (the night being cold in October), and there we remained till daylight. Then one of the company knew the place to be Cooper's Creek, a little above Philadelphia, which we saw as soon as we got out of the creek; and arrived there about eight or nine o'clock on the Sunday morning and landed at the Market Street wharf.

I have been the more particular in this description of my journey, and shall be so of my first entry into that city, that you may in your mind compare such unlikely beginnings with the figure I have since made there. I was in my working dress, my best clothes being to come round by sea. I was dirty from my journey; my pockets were stuffed out with shirts and stockings; I knew no soul, nor where to look for lodging. Fatigued with walking, rowing, and want of sleep, I was very hungry, and my whole stock of cash consisted of a Dutch dollar and about a shilling in copper coin, which I gave to the boatmen for my passage. At first they refused it on account of my having rowed, but I insisted on their taking it. A man is sometimes more generous when he has little money than when he has plenty, perhaps through fear of being thought to have but little. I walked towards the top of the street, gazing about till near Market Street, where I met a boy with bread. I have often made a meal of dry bread and, inquiring where he had bought it, I went immediately to the baker's he directed me to. I asked for biscuit, meaning such as we had in Boston, but that sort, it seems, was not made in Philadelphia. I then asked for a threepenny loaf and was told they had none such. Not knowing the different prices nor the names of the different sorts of bread, I told him to give me three pennyworth of any sort. He gave me accordingly three great puffy rolls. I was surprised at the quantity but took it, and having no room in my pockets, walked off with a roll under each arm and eating the other. Thus I went up Market Street as far as Fourth Street, passing by the door of Mr. Read, my future wife's father, when she, standing at the door, saw me and thought I made – as I certainly did – a most awkward, ridiculous appearance. Then I turned and went down Chestnut Street and part of Waltnut Street, eating my roll all the way, and, coming round, found myself again at Market Street wharf near the boat I came in, to which I went for a draught of the river water. And, being filled with one of my rolls, gave the other two to a woman and her child that came down the river in the boat with us and were waiting to go farther. Thus refreshed, I walked again up the street, which by this time had many clean dressed people in it who were all walking the same way. I joined them, and thereby was led into the great meetinghouse of the Quakers near the market. I sat down among them and, after looking round awhile and hearing nothing said, being very drowsy through labour and want of rest the preceding night, I fell fast asleep and continued so till the meeting broke up, when someone was kind enough to rouse me. This was therefore the first house I was in, or slept in, in Philadelphia.

Original MS of autobiography in Huntington Library. Many editions available. Best scholarly ed. *Benjamin Franklin's Memoirs*, ed. M. Farrand (1949). Above text based on early eds. collated with Farrand ed.

VIII

PLANS OF UNION; GRIEVANCES AGAINST ENGLAND

1   Frontier Rebellion, 1676

Colonists on the frontier frequently suffered from Indian attacks and rarely could count on adequate protection from the government of the colony. For example, Pennsylvanians protested in vain to the Quaker government in Philadelphia about Indian forays against frontier outposts. In 1676 Nathaniel Bacon, an Englishman who had recently taken up land in the interior of Virginia, led a rebellion against Governor William Berkeley and his governing clique, not only because of Berkeley's failure to protect the frontier but because of other grievances as well. Bacon's statement concerning these grievances follows.

If virtue be a sin, if piety be guilt, all the principles of morality, goodness and justice be perverted, we must confess that those who are now called rebels may be in danger of those high imputations. . . . Now let us compare these things together and see what sponges have sucked up the public treasure, and whether it has not been privately contrived away by unworthy favourites and juggling parasites whose tottering fortunes have been repaired and supported at the public charge. Now if it be so, judge what greater guilt can be than to offer to pry into these and to unriddle the mysterious wiles of a powerful cabal; let all people judge what can be of more dangerous import than to suspect the so long safe proceedings of some of our grandees, and whether people may with safety open their eyes in so nice a concern. . . .

Judge, therefore, all wise and unprejudiced men who may or can faithfully or truly with an honest heart, attempt the country's good, their vindication, and liberty without the aspersion of traitor and rebel, since as so doing they must of necessity gall such tender and dear concerns. But to manifest sincerity and loyalty to the world, and how much we abhor those bitter names; may all the world know that we do unanimously desire to represent our sad and heavy grievances to his most sacred Majesty as our refuge and sanctuary, where we do well know that all our causes will be impartially heard and equal justice administered to all men.

THE DECLARATION OF THE PEOPLE

For having upon specious pretences of public works, raised unjust taxes upon the commonalty for the advancement of private favourites and other sinister ends, but no visible effects in any measure adequate.

For not having during the long time of his government in any measure advanced this hopeful colony, either by fortification, towns or trade.

For having abused and rendered contemptible the majesty of justice, of advancing to places of judicature scandalous and ignorant favourites.

For having wronged his Majesty's prerogative and interest by assuming the monopoly of the beaver trade.

By having in that unjust gain bartered and sold his Majesty's country and the lives of his loyal subjects to the barbarous heathen.

For having protected, favoured and emboldened the Indians against his Majesty's most loyal subjects, never contriving, requiring, or appointing any due or proper means of satisfaction for their many invasions, murders, and robberies committed upon us.

For having, when the army of the English was just upon the track of the Indians, which now in all places burn, spoil, and murder, and when we might with ease have destroyed them who then were in open hostility, for having expressly countermanded and sent back our army by passing his word for the peaceable demeanour of the said Indians, who immediately prosecuted their evil intentions, committing horrid murders and robberies in all places. . . .

For having with only the privacy of some few favourites, without acquainting the people, only by the alteration of a figure, forged a commission by we know not what hand, not only without but against the consent of the people, for raising and effecting of civil wars and distractions, which being happily and without bloodshed prevented.

For having the second time attempted the same thereby calling down our forces from the defence of the frontiers, and most weak exposed places, for the prevention of civil mischief and ruin amongst ourselves, whilst the barbarous enemy in all places did invade, murder, and spoil us, his Majesty's most faithful subjects.

Of these, the aforesaid articles, we accuse Sir William Berkeley, as guilty of each and every one of the same, and as one who has traitorously attempted, violated and injured his Majesty's interest here, by the loss of a great part of his colony, and many of his faithful and loyal subjects by him betrayed, and in a barbarous and shameful manner exposed to the incursions and murders of the heathen.

And we further declare these, the ensuing persons in this list, to have been his wicked, and pernicious counsellors, aiders and assisters against the commonalty in these our cruel commotions:

[LIST OF NAMES]

And we do further demand, that the said Sir William Berkeley, with all the persons in this list, be forthwith delivered up, or surrender themselves, within four days after the notice hereof, or otherwise we declare as followeth: that in whatsoever house, place, or ship any of the said persons shall reside, be hid, or protected, we do declare that the owners, masters, or inhabitants of the said places, to be confederates and traitors to the people, and the estates of them, as also of all the aforesaid persons, to be confiscated. This we, the commons of Virginia, do declare desiring a prime union amongst ourselves, that we may jointly, and with one accord defend ourselves against the common enemy. And let not the faults of the guilty be the reproach of the innocent, or the faults or crimes of the oppressors divide and separate us, who have suffered by their oppressions.

These are therefore in his Majesty's name, to command you forthwith to seize the persons above mentioned as traitors to the king and country, and them to bring to Middle Plantation, and there to secure them, till further order, and in case of opposition, if you want any other assistance, you are forthwith to demand it in the name of the people of all the counties of Virginia.

NATH BACON, Gen'l.
By the Consent of the People.
Printed in *The Virginia Magazine of History and Biography*, I (1894), pp. 55-61

2   William Penn's Proposal for Colonial Unity, 1697

One of the earliest proposals for a union of the British colonies was made by William Penn but nothing came of it. Others also saw the need of unity but no one could persuade the colonies to join, even for mutual defence.

A brief and plain scheme how the English colonies in the North parts of America, – viz., Boston, Connecticut, Rhode Island, New York, New Jerseys, Pennsylvania, Maryland, Virginia, and Carolina, – may be made more useful to the crown and one another's peace and safety with an universal concurrence.

1. That the several colonies before mentioned do meet once a year, and oftener if need be during the war, and at least once in two years in times of peace, by their stated and appointed deputies, to debate and resolve of such measures as are most advisable for their better understanding and the public tranquillity and safety.

2. That, in order to it, two persons, well qualified for sense, sobriety, and substance, be appointed by each province as their representatives or deputies, which in the whole make the congress to consist of twenty persons.

3. That the king's commissioner, for that purpose specially appointed, shall have the chair and preside in the said congress.

4. That they shall meet as near as conveniently may to the most central colony for ease of the deputies.

5. Since that may in all probability be New York, both because it is near the centre of the colonies and for that it is a frontier and in the king's nomination, the governor of that colony may therefore also be the king's high commissioner during the session, after the manner of Scotland.

6. That their business shall be to hear and adjust all matters of complaint or difference between province and province. As, 1st, where persons quit their own province and go to another, that they may avoid their just debts, though they be able to pay them; 2d, where offenders fly justice, or justice cannot well be had upon such offenders in the provinces that entertain them; 3d, to prevent or cure injuries in point of commerce; 4th, to consider the ways and means to support the

union and safety of these provinces against the public enemies. In which congress the quotas of men and charges will be much easier and more equally set than it is possible for any establishment made here to do; for the provinces, knowing their own condition and one another's, can debate that matter with more freedom and satisfaction, and better adjust and balance their affairs in all respects for their common safety.

7. That, in times of war, the king's high commissioner shall be general or chief commander of the several quotas upon service against the common enemy, as he shall be advised, for the good and benefit of the whole.

*Documents Relative to the Colonial History of
... New York,* ed. E. B. O'Callaghan (1856-
83), iv.296-7

3   Need for Unity under Royal Authority, 1701

The anonymous colonial who wrote *An Essay upon the Government of the English Plantations on the Continent of America* (1701) saw clearly the difficulties suffered by the colonies because of their disparity in government, their lack of unity, and their weakness in the face of attack. His remedy was unification under the authority of the English sovereign.

... The King's governors in the plantations either have, or pretend to have, very large powers within their provinces which, together with the trusts reposed in them of disposing of all places of honour and profit, and of being chief judges in the supreme courts of judicature ... render them so absolute that it is almost impossible to lay any sort of restraint upon them.

On the other side, in some of the proprieties the hands of the government are so feeble that they cannot protect themselves against the insolencies of the common people, which makes them very subject to anarchy and confusion. ...

Another very considerable difficulty the plantations lie under from their governors is that there is no way left to represent their evil treatment to the King. For nothing of that nature can be done without money, no money can be had without an Assembly, and the governor always hath a negative in their proceedings; and not only so ... he can let alone calling one or, being called, can dissolve them at pleasure.

But the last and greatest unhappiness the plantations labour under is that the King and court of England are altogether strangers to the true state of affairs in America, for that is the true cause why their grievances have not been long since redressed. . . .

THE GOVERNMENT OF ALL THE PLANTATIONS TO BE ANNEXED TO THE CROWN

For the better regulation and management of these plantations, it is humbly proposed that the government of them all may be annexed to the Crown by act of Parliment, for without that it will be impossible to keep them upon an equal foot; but some tricks or other will be played by the charter governments, let their pretensions be never so fair. . . .

I am not ignorant that many persons whose interests are concerned will look upon this as . . . very much tending to the destruction of property, and the like. To all which I shall make but little answer, and that in this manner:

1. That in the beginning Virginia was planted by a company, who had a charter for their so doing; and afterwards . . . not only the government but the very property of the land was taken into the King's hands and so remains at this day.

The government of Maryland is now in the King's hands, and yet the Lord Baltimore enjoys his property in the land as he did heretofore, and not only so, but all other revenues that were settled on him by the Assembly of that province.

The government of New England is now in the King's hands; and if the public welfare required it, why should not the proprieties of Pennsylvania, the Jerseys, and the Carolinas be likewise governed in the same manner?

2. The propriety of the soil may remain to the proprietor, as heretofore, and need not be prejudiced by the King's appointing governours in those parts. And if this be not satisfactory, but they still pretend to have the governments entirely in their own hands, I beg leave to admonish them to consult with their own counselors at law how far the King hath power to grant the supreme government of the plantations to any person or persons, and their heirs, without the assent of Parliament.

I shall say no more to this point at present; though it may very reasonably be urged that in times of danger England must be at the charge to defend them all, which cannot well be done without taking the government.

That it is necessary for all the colonies to be united under one head for their common defence; and that it will be much more so if the French, or any other nation, possess themselves of the River Mississippi and the lakes to the westward. That in case of a war with Spain nothing could tend more to the advantage of England than having all these colonies under the Crown, to give such assistance as should be necessary towards any design upon the West Indies, which would never be done by the proprieties unless they saw some extraordinary private advantage by it. . . .

THE KING AND COURT OF ENGLAND UNACQUAINTED WITH THE STATE OF THE PLANTATIONS

1. That every colony have an agent constantly residing in England to give an account from time to time, as he shall be thereto required, of all the affairs and transactions of the plantation he is authorized by. And lest this agent be corrupted and wrought upon to give wrong informations, as a check upon him:

2. Let one person be commissioned from England to travel through all the plantations to make inquiry into, and give a true representation of, the state of their affairs. And these two persons, being checks one upon the other, would both of them be obliged to speak the truth. . . .

By these means it is probable the King and court of England may be made thoroughly sensible of the true state of affairs in this remote part of the world which, it is presumed, will be the first and greatest step towards remedying any former mismanagements.

> *An Essay upon the Government of the English Plantations on the Continent of America* (1701), ed. L. B. Wright (1945), pp. 36–56 *passim*

4   Franklin's Plan of Union, 1754

Benjamin Franklin drew up a plan for a confederation of the British colonies in North America. This plan, presented at a congress of representatives from various colonies, called at Albany in 1754, was earnestly advocated by Franklin, who had previously published in his paper, *The Pennsylvania Gazette*, a famous cartoon of a snake cut into segments, with the legend, 'Join or Die'. But when the proposal was presented to the colonial assemblies, not one would sacrifice any of its prerogatives in order to join a confederation.

It is proposed that humble application be made for an act of Parliament of Great Britain, by virtue of which one general government may be formed in America, including all the said colonies, within and under which government each colony may retain its present constitution, except in the particulars wherein a change may be directed by the said act, as hereafter follows.

1. That the said general government be administered by a President-General, to be appointed and supported by the crown; and a Grand Council, to be chosen by the representatives of the people of the several Colonies met in their respective assemblies.

2. That within ——— months after the passing such act, the House of Representatives that happen to be sitting within that time, or that shall be especially for that purpose convened, may and shall choose members for the Grand Council, in the following proportion, that is to say,

Massachusetts Bay	7
New Hampshire	2
Connecticut	5
Rhode Island	2
New York	4
New Jersey	3
Pennsylvania	6
Maryland	4
Virginia	7
North Carolina	4
South Carolina	4
	48

3.——— who shall meet for the first time at the city of Philadelphia, being called by the President-General as soon as conveniently may be after his appointment.

4. That there shall be a new election of the members of the Grand Council every three years; and, on the death or resignation of any member, his place should be supplied by a new choice at the next sitting of the Assembly of the Colony he represented.

5. That after the first three years, when the proportion of money arising out of each Colony to the general treasury can be known, the number of members to be chosen for each Colony shall, from time to time, in all ensuing elections, be regulated by that proportion, yet so as that the number to be chosen by any one Province be not more than seven, nor less than two.

6. That the Grand Council shall meet once in every year, and oftener if occasion require, at such time and place as they shall adjourn to at the last preceding meeting, or as they shall be called to meet at by the President-General on any emergency; he having first obtained in writing the consent of seven of the members to such call, and sent duly and timely notice to the whole.

7. That the Grand Council have power to choose their speaker; and shall neither be dissolved, prorogued, nor continued sitting longer than six weeks at one time, without their own consent or the special command of the crown.

8. That the members of the Grand Council shall be allowed for their service ten shillings sterling per diem, during their session and journey to and from the place of meeting; twenty miles to be reckoned a day's journey.

9. That the assent of the President-General be requisite to all acts of the Grand Council, and that it be his office and duty to cause them to be carried into execution.

10. That the President-General, with the advice of the Grand Council, hold or direct all Indian treaties, in which the general interest of the Colonies may be concerned; and make peace or declare war with Indian nations.

11. That they make such laws as they judge necesary for regulating all Indian trade.

12. That they make all purchases from Indians, for the crown, of lands not now within the bounds of particular Colonies, or that shall not be within their bounds when some of them are reduced to more convenient dimensions.

13. That they make new settlements on such purchases, by granting lands in the King's name, reserving a quitrent to the crown for the use of the general treasury.

14. That they make laws for regulating and governing such new settlements, till the crown shall think fit to form them into particular governments.

15. That they raise and pay soldiers and build forts for the defence of any of the Colonies, and equip vessels of force to guard the coasts and protect the trade on the ocean, lakes, or great rivers; but they shall not impress men in any Colony, without the consent of the Legislature.

16. That for these purposes they have power to make laws, and lay and levy such general duties, imposts, or taxes, as to them shall appear most equal and just (considering the ability and other circumstances of the inhabitants in the several Colonies), and such as may be collected with the least inconvenience to the people; rather discouraging luxury, than loading industry with unnecessary burdens.

17. That they may appoint a General Treasurer and Particular Treasurer in each government when necessary; and, from time to time, may order the sums in the treasuries of each government into the general treasury; or draw on them for special payments, as they find most convenient.

18. Yet no money to issue but by joint orders of the President-General and Grand Council; except where sums have been appropriated to particular purposes, and the President-General is previously empowered by an act to draw such sums.

19. That the general accounts shall be yearly settled and reported to the several Assemblies.

20. That a quorum of the Grand Council, empowered to act with the President-General, do consist of twenty-five members; among whom there shall be one or more from a majority of the Colonies.

21. That the laws made by them for the purposes aforesaid shall not be repugnant, but, as near as may be, agreeable to the laws of England, and shall be transmitted to the King in Council for approbation, as soon as may be after their passing; and if not disapproved within three years after presentation, to remain in force.

22. That, in case of the death of the President-General, the Speaker of the Grand Council for the time being shall succeed, and be vested with the same powers and authorities, to continue till the King's pleasure be known.

23. That all military commission officers, whether for land or sea

service, to act under this general constitution, shall be nominated by the President-General; but the approbation of the Grand Council is to be obtained, before they receive their commissions. And all civil officers are to be nominated by the Grand Council, and to receive the President-General's approbation before they officiate.

24. But, in case of vacancy by death or removal of any officer, civil or military, under this constitution, the Governor of the Province in which such vacancy happens may appoint, till the pleasure of the President-General and Grand Council can be known.

25. That the particular military as well as civil establishments in each Colony remain in their present state, the general constitution notwithstanding; and that on sudden emergencies any Colony may defend itself and lay the accounts of expense thence arising before the President-General and General Council, who may allow and order payment of the same, as far as they judge such accounts just and reasonable.

Works of Benjamin Franklin, ed. J. Sparks (1840), iii.36ff.

5 The Stamp Act, 1765

The Stamp Act, passed on 22 March 1765, put a tax on practically every type of paper used in business, legal documents, pamphlets, newspapers, and even almanacs. No act could have been designed to offend more articulate people in the colonies than this revenue bill.

An act for granting and applying certain stamp duties, and other duties, in the British colonies and plantations in America, towards further defraying the expenses of defending, protecting, and securing the same; and for amending such parts of the several acts of parliament relating to the trade and revenues of the said colonies and plantations, as direct the manner of determining and recovering the penalties and forfeitures therein mentioned.

WHEREAS by an act made in the last session of parliament, several duties were granted, continued, and appropriated towards defraying the expenses of defending, protecting, and securing, the British colonies and plantations in America: and whereas it is just and necessary that provision be made for raising a further revenue within Your Majesty's dominions in America, towards defraying the said expenses: . . . Be it enacted . . . that from and after the first day of November, one thousand seven hundred and sixty-five, there shall be raised, levied, collected, and paid unto his Majesty, his heirs, and successors, throughout the colonies and plantations in America which now are, or hereafter may be, under the dominion of his Majesty, his heirs and successors:

For every skin or piece of vellum or parchment, or sheet or piece of paper, on which shall be engrossed, written or printed, any declaration, plea, replication, rejoinder, demurrer, or other pleading, or any copy thereof, in any court of law within the British colonies and plantations in America, a stamp duty of three pence. . . .

And be it further enacted . . . that all books and pamphlets serving chiefly for the purpose of an almanac, by whatsoever name or names intituled or described, are and shall be charged with the duty imposed by this act on almanacs, but not with any of the duties charged by this act on pamphlets, or other printed papers. . . .

Statutes at Large, ed. Pickering, xxvi.179ff.

6   Stamp Act Unconstitutional, 1766

A court in Northampton County, Virginia, reviewed the Stamp Act, and on 11 February 1766 declared it unconstitutional.

Williamsburg, March 21. The following is a copy of a late order of Northampton Court, on the eastern shore of this colony, which we are desired to insert. At a court held for Northampton county, Feb. 11, 1766:

'On the motion of the Clerk and other Officers of this Court, praying their opinion whether the act entitled "An Act for granting and applying certain Stamp Duties, and other Duties in America, &c," was binding on the inhabitants of this colony, and whether they the said Officers should incur any penalties by not using stamped paper, agreeable to the directions of the said act, the Court unanimously declared it to be their opinion that the said act did not bind, affect or concern the inhabitants of this colony, in as much as they conceive the same to be unconstitutional, and that the said several officers may proceed to the execution of their respective offices without incurring any penalties by means thereof; which opinion this court doth order to be recorded. Griffin Stith, C.N.C.'

From the *Virginia Gazette*, 21 March 1766.
Reprinted in *Documents of American History*,
ed. H. S. Commager (1940), p. 59

7   The Quartering Act, 1765

Among the laws passed during the controversies that led to the final break with Great Britain in 1776, only the Stamp Act caused more irritation than the Quartering Act, which required each colony to furnish food and drink to British troops stationed within its borders and to see that proper quarters were available. The refusal of the colonies to comply with this law caused much bitterness.

Whereas in and by an Act made in the present session of Parliament entitled, *An Act for punishing mutiny and desertion*, and for the better payment of the army and their quarters: several regulations are made and enacted for the better government of the army, and their observing strict discipline, and for providing quarters for the army, and carriages on marches and other necessary occasions, and inflicting penalties on offenders against the same Act, and for many other good purposes therein mentioned; but the same may not be sufficient for the forces that may be employed in his Majesty's dominions in America; and whereas, during the continuance of the said Act there may be occasion for marching and quartering of regiments and companies of his Majesty's forces in several parts of his Majesty's dominions in America; and whereas the public houses and barracks in his Majesty's dominions in America may not be sufficient to supply quarters for such forces; and whereas it is expedient and necessary that carriages and other conveniences, upon the march of troops in his Majesty's dominions in America should be supplied for that purpose: be it enacted . . . that for and during the continuance of this Act, and no longer, it shall and may be lawful to and for the constables, tithingmen, magistrates, and other civil officers of villages, towns, townships, cities, districts, and other places, within his Majesty's dominions in America, and in their default or absence, for any one justice of the peace inhabiting in or near any such village, township, city, district, or place, and for no others; and such constables, tithingmen, magistrates, and other civil officers as aforesaid, are hereby required to quarter and billet the officers and soldiers in his Majesty's service, in the barracks provided by the colonies; and if there shall not be sufficient room in the said barracks for the officers and soldiers, then and in such case only, to quarter and billet the residue of such officers and soldiers for whom there shall not be room in such barracks, in inns, livery stables, ale-houses, victualling houses, and the houses of sellers of wine by retail to be drunk in their own houses or places thereunto belonging, and all houses of persons selling of rum, brandy, strong water, cider, or metheglin, by retail, to be drunk in houses; and in case there shall not be sufficient room for the officers and soldiers in such barracks, inns, victualling and other public ale-houses, that in such and no other case, and upon no other account, it shall and may be lawful for the governor and council of each respective province in his Majesty's dominions in America, to authorize and appoint, and they are hereby directed and empowered to authorize and appoint such proper person or persons as they shall think fit, to take, hire and make fit, and, in default of the said governor and council appointing and authorizing such person or persons, or in default of such person or persons so appointed neglecting or refusing to do their duty, in that case it shall and may be lawful for any two or more of his Majesty's justices of the peace in or near the said villages, towns, townships, cities, districts, and other places, and they are hereby required to take, hire, and make fit for the reception of his Majesty's forces, such and so many uninhabited houses, outhouses, barns, or other buildings, as shall be necessary, to quarter therein the residue of such officers and soldiers for whom there should not be room in such barracks and public houses as aforesaid, and to put and quarter the residue of such officers and soldiers therein.

VII. And whereas there are several barracks in several places in his Majesty's said dominions in America, or some of them, provided by the colonies, for the lodging and covering of soldiers in lieu of quarters, for the ease and conveniency as well of the inhabitants of and in such colonies, as of the soldiers; it is hereby further enacted, that all such officers and soldiers so put and placed in such barracks, or in hired uninhabited houses, outhouses, barns, or other buildings, shall, from time to time be furnished and supplied there by the persons to be authorized or appointed for that purpose by the governor and council of each respective province, or upon neglect or refusal of such governor and council in any province, then by two or more justices of the peace residing in or near such place, with fire, candles, vinegar, and salt, bedding, utensils for dressing their victuals, and small beer or cider, not exceeding five pints, or half a pint of rum mixed with a quart of water, to each man, without paying anything for the same.

VIII. And that the several persons who shall so take, hire, and fit up as aforesaid, such uninhabited houses, outhouses, barns, or other buildings, for the reception of the officers and soldiers, and who shall so furnish the same, and also the said barracks with fire, candles, vinegar, and salt, bedding, utensils for dressing victuals, and small beer and cider, or rum, as aforesaid, may be reimbursed and paid all such charges and expenses they shall be put to therein, be it enacted by the authority aforesaid, that the respective provinces shall pay unto such person or persons all such sum or sums of money so by them paid, laid out, or expended, for the takings, hiring, and fitting up such uninhabited houses, outhouses, barns, or other buildings, and for furnishing the officers and soldiers therein, and in the barracks with fire, candles, vinegar, and salt, bedding, utensils for dressing victuals, and small beer, cider, or rum, as aforesaid: and such sum or sums are hereby required to be raised in such manner as the public charges for the provinces respectively are raised.

Statutes at Large, ed. Pickering, xxvi.305-9

8   The Proclamation of 1763

After the Peace of Paris, the British government sought to stabilize the fur trade and confirm the Indians west of the Allegheny Mountains in their rights to hunting grounds. To accomplish this the King issued the famous Proclamation of 1763 forbidding settlement beyond the crest of the mountains.

Whereas we have taken into our royal consideration the extensive and valuable acquisitions in America, secured to our crown by the late definitive treaty of peace concluded at Paris the 10th day of February last, and being desirous that all our loving subjects, as well of our kingdoms as of our colonies in America, may avail themselves, with all convenient speed, of the great benefits and advantages which must accrue therefrom to their commerce, manufactures, and navigation; we have thought fit, with the advice of our Privy Council, to issue this our royal proclamation, hereby to publish and declare to all our loving subjects, that we have, with the advice of our said Privy Council, granted our letters patent under our great seal of Great Britain, to erect within the countries and islands, ceded and confirmed to us by the said treaty, four distinct and separate governments, styled and called by the names of Quebec, East Florida, West Florida, and Grenada. . . . [Here follows a passage describing the boundaries of these territories.]

And to the end that the open and free fishery of our subjects may be extended to, and carried on upon, the coast of Labrador and the adjacent islands, we have thought fit, with the advice of our said Privy Council, to put all that coast, from the river St. John's to Hudson's Straits, together with the islands of Anticosti and Magdalen, and all other smaller islands lying upon the said coast, under the care and inspection of our governor of Newfoundland.

We have also, with the advice of our Privy Council, thought fit to annex the islands of St. John and Cape Breton, or Isle Royale, with the lesser islands adjacent thereto, to our government of Nova Scotia.

We have also, with the advice of our Privy Council aforesaid, annexed to our province of Georgia, all the lands lying between the rivers Altamaha and St. Mary's. . . .

[A passage on the establishment of courts in the several regions is omitted.]

We have also thought fit, with the advice of our Privy Council as aforesaid, to give unto the governors and councils of our said three new colonies upon the continent, full power and authority to settle and agree with the inhabitants of our said new colonies, or with any other persons who shall resort thereto, for such lands, tenements, and hereditaments, as are now, or hereafter shall be, in our power to dispose of, and them to grant to any such person or persons, upon such terms, and under such moderate quit-rents, services, and acknowledgments, as have been appointed and settled in our other colonies, and under such conditions as shall appear to us to be necessary and expedient for the advantage of the grantees, and the improvement and settlement of our said colonies.

And whereas we are desirous, upon all occasions, to testify our royal sense and approbation of the conduct and bravery of the officers and soldiers of our armies, and to reward the same, we do hereby command and impower our governors of our said three new colonies, and all other our governors of our several provinces on the continent of North America, to grant, without fee or reward, to such reduced officers as have served in North America during the late war, and to such private soldiers as have been or shall be disbanded in America, and are actually residing there, and shall personally apply for the same, the following quantities of lands, subject, at the expiration of ten years, to the same quit-rents as other lands are subject to in the province within which they are granted, as also subject to the same conditions of cultivation and improvement, viz.

To every person having the rank of a field officer, five thousand acres. To every captain, three thousand acres. To every subaltern or staff officer, two thousand acres. To every non-commission officer, two hundred acres. To every private man, fifty acres.

We do likewise authorize and require the governors and commanders-in-chief of all our said colonies upon the continent of North America to grant the like quantities of land, and upon the same conditions, to such reduced officers of our navy of like rank, as served on board our ships of war in North America at the times of the reduction of Louisburg and Quebec in the late war, and who shall personally apply to our respective governors for such grants.

And whereas it is just and reasonable, and essential to our interest, and the security of our colonies, that the several nations or tribes of Indians with whom we are connected, and who live under our protection, should not be molested or disturbed in the possession of such parts of our dominions and territories as, not having been ceded to, or purchased by us, are reserved to them, or any of them, as their hunting grounds; we do therefore, with the advice of our Privy Council, declare it to be our royal will and pleasure, that no governor, or commander-in-chief, in any of our colonies of Quebec, East Florida, or West Florida, do presume, upon any pretence whatever, to grant warrants of survey, or pass any patents for lands beyond the bounds of their respective governments, as described in their commissions; as also that no governor or commander-in-chief in any of our other colonies or plantations in America, do presume for the present, and until our further pleasure be known, to grant warrants of survey, or pass patents for any lands beyond the heads or sources of any of the rivers which fall into the Atlantic Ocean from the west and northwest; or upon any lands whatever, which not having been ceded to, or purchased by us, as aforesaid, are reserved to the said Indians, or any of them.

And we do further declare it to be our royal will and pleasure, for the present, as aforesaid, to reserve under our sovereignty, protection, and dominion, for the use of the said Indians, all the lands and territories not included within the limits of our said three new governments, or within the limits of the territory granted to the Hudson's Bay Company, as also all the lands and territories lying to the westward of the sources of the rivers which fall into the sea from the west and northwest as aforesaid; and we do hereby strictly forbid, on pain of our displeasure, all our loving subjects from making any purchases or settlements whatever, or taking possession of any of the lands above reserved, without our especial leave and licence for that purpose first obtained.

And we do further strictly enjoin and require all persons whatever, who have either wilfully or inadvertently seated themselves upon any lands within the countries above described, or upon any other lands, which not having been ceded to, or purchased by us, are still reserved to the said Indians as aforesaid, forthwith to remove themselves from such settlements.

And whereas great frauds and abuses have been committed in the purchasing lands of the Indians, to the great prejudice of our interests, and to the great dissatisfaction of the said Indians; in order, therefore, to prevent such irregularities for the future, and to the end that the Indians may be convinced of our justice and determined resolution to remove all reasonable cause of discontent, we do, with the advice of our Privy Council, strictly enjoin and require, that no private person do presume to make any purchase from the said Indians of any lands reserved to the said Indians within those parts of our colonies where we have thought proper to allow settlement; but that if at any time any of the said Indians should be inclined to dispose of the said lands, the same shall be purchased only for us, in our name, at some public meeting or assembly of the said Indians, to be held for that purpose by the governor or commander-in-chief of our colonies respectively within which they shall lie: and in case they shall lie within the limits of any proprietary government, they shall be purchased only for the use and in the name of such proprietaries, conformable to such directions and instructions as we or they shall think proper to give for that purpose: and we do, by the advice of our Privy Council, declare and enjoin, that the trade with the said Indians shall be free and open to all our subjects whatever, provided that every person who may incline to trade with the said Indians, do take out a licence for carrying on such trade, from the governor or commander-in-chief of any of our colonies respectively, where such person shall reside, and also give security to observe such regulations as we shall at any time think fit, by ourselves or by our commissaries, to be appointed for this purpose, to direct and appoint for the benefit of the said trade; and we do hereby authorize, enjoin, and require the governors and commanders-in-chief of all our colonies respectively, as well those under our immediate government, as those under the government and direction of proprietaries, to grant such licences without fee or reward, taking especial care to insert therein a condition that such licence shall be void, and the security forfeited, in case the person to whom the same is granted, shall refuse or neglect to observe such regulations as we shall think proper to prescribe as aforesaid.

And we do further expressly enjoin and require all officers whatever, as well military as those employed in the management and direction of Indian affairs within the territories reserved, as aforesaid, for the use of the said Indians, to seize and apprehend all persons whatever, who standing charged with treasons, misprisions of treason, murders, or other felonies or misdemeanours, shall fly from justice and take refuge in the said territory, and to send them under a proper guard to the colony where the crime was committed of which they stand accused, in order to take their trial for the same.

Given at our court at St. James's, the seventh day of October, one thousand seven hundred and sixty three, in the third year of our reign.

British Royal Proclamations Relating to America, 1603-1783, ed. C. S. Brigham (1911), pp. 212-18